HIDDEN

LANGUAGE

CODES

**discard a weak language of doubt and
excuse and acquire a vocabulary
of power and sovereignty**

R. NEVILLE JOHNSTON

WEISERBOOKS
Boston, MA/York Beach, ME

First published in 2005 by
Red Wheel/Weiser, LLC
York Beach, ME
With offices at:
368 Congress Street
Boston, MA 02210
www.redwheelweiser.com

Library of Congress Cataloging-in-Publication Data
Johnston, R. Neville.
Hidden language codes / R. Neville Johnston.
p. cm.
Includes bibliographical references.
ISBN 1-57863-362-1
1. Self-actualization (Psychology)—Miscellanea.   2. Language and
languages—Miscellanea.   I. Title.
BF1045.S44J64 2005
131—dc22   2005018867

Typeset in Berkeley by Kathryn Sky-Peck
Printed in Canada
TCP
12 11 10 09 08 07 06 05
8 7 6 5 4 3 2 1

LOVE IS THE SINGLE MOTIVATION THERE IS. No matter what happens to a child, the child regards the experience as love. If it is sweet care, then this is love. If it is abuse, then abuse is love. No matter what any adult is doing, they are acting out what they have been taught is love. Imagine understanding that no matter what anyone is doing, it is an act of love. The object then becomes to choose the higher expression of love.

There is no human being on this planet to whom you are not directly related. Wherever you walk, walk among your family. It is in the spirit of dedication that I ask that you give this book to the person you love, or the person who is playing the part of your worthy opponent. Either way, in sharing this book, you get to live on a planet that is more evolved.

Many have assisted me in the commitment to ignite this book. For this there is surely gratitude, and so this is dedicated to: us, our family of humanity. To my daughters, Grace and Caramai, and their mother Ariane. Mary Phelan is adored for the support she has given me both as editor and companion. Thank you, dear reader, for the self-love involved in the reading of this volume. It is to the all, that I'm dedicated in service.

Contents

QUADRANT 4
ARCHETYPE UPGRADE

Acknowledgments

Our movement forward, our evolution, is designed as the "buddy system." As we become more enlightened, we awaken those around us. There are none among us who don't stand on the shoulders of our ancestors.

I acknowledge and thank my teachers, everyone I have ever met, throughout all the sands of time. Know that I hold each of us dear!

Preface

One day in late spring of 1977 I am with a beautiful actress. We are leaving the theater where we are thespians. Then suddenly . . .

I am shot to death. A man, a total stranger, appears right in front of us with a gun. He shoots me three times. I'll hear those shots for the rest of my life. It is the one that hits my head that turns out to be fatal.

Earlier I am feeling very good, looking forward to the next adventure the evening will hold. The night air is very warm and (pardon the pun) "muggy." As we approach the top steps of this literally underground theater, a man comes straight toward us, a chrome pistol in his hand.

Thinking it is a robbery, I begin to reach for my wallet. The next thing I know I am looking at a hole in my new silk shirt. Time stops. Looking at the wound, my brain is saying "Look, that's the dermas, epidermis. Yuck, a fatty layer, muscle. Wow, I have a muscle! That dark hole must be the inside of my stomach. Wow, that hole is in me . . ."

Time starts again. I look up to see what is happening. A second bullet hits my hip, and ricochets down inside my left leg. It is still there today. Where is this coming from? As I look in the direction that the first two bullets have come from, I see hairs from my head falling in front of my eyes.

The bullet that impacts my cranium cuts the follicles as it passes through the skull. I feel the warm gush of blood flooding down my forehead. I feel zero pain.

This stranger is running away. I am standing there watching him disappear into the crowd by the entrance to the theater. I look down to see a body lying there. It is wearing my clothes, lying in a puddle of blood, no breath, no discernable eye movement. Hmm . . .

It's me! I am thinking to my self, "Gee, this is the best astral projection that I've ever done. Ah . . . this may not be the best time to be astrally projecting; there may be some restriction on getting back into my body."

I realize that there is an alarm bell sounding. In fact, very loudly. Hmm . . . That's my old high school fire drill alarm . . . Ringing here? As if this theater has an employee who's job is to ring bells whenever anyone gets shot. Upon my realization the bell stops.

The next thought is, "dust collects up." I never realized that dust collects on the ceiling. I know this because it tickles my nose as I rise through it. The next thing I know, I'm in a room filled with light.

During the entire experience, my stream of conscious thought never stops. Not once; it remains unbroken. People associate death with this big off switch . . . Ah, not so much.

Because there is a brain between me and the white light, the light becomes an angel. Over the years I have done a lot of research into "near" death experiences. I never experience the tunnel that people talk about. The tunnel is an illusion that is created by looking at the light and then looking all around. What are ya looking for, a brighter light? I am just there, in the light as an automatic process.

Which being we meet after death has to do with our individual belief system. It might be Charon with the ferry across the River Styx if you were an ancient Greek. Grandpa or an elder clan member if you worshiped ancestors in the Chinese or Native American traditions. Shamans who have passed over will take on the role of next-world greeter in many tribal cultures. Whomever you meet, it will be someone with whom you feel perfectly safe.

The being that is greeting me has the clearest blue eyes I've ever seen. Let's call him St. Peter. He is literally looking through a book. The book is the story of my life. You can throw out the expression "permanent record"—the concept that is used to threaten school children—there is no such thing. Yet we do indeed register our signature in the universe with everything we do.

I immediately begin the "guilty dance" saying, "I may not have done the best possible job down there, given my talents and the circumstances. Besides, I'm an only child and if my mother hears that I've been shot down this way, it could kill her. Is there something that can be done?"

He holds up his hand in the classic "stop," and says, "Chill, Dude." My angels speak to me in street vernacular.

I immediately cease the guilty dance and am silent. A great calm comes over me. It starts in my heart and radiates out through my body/being. Even to this very day I remain "chillin'."

He explains that the life I have just lived was like a suit of clothes. It could easily be laid aside, meaning that this is just one facet in the crystal of my central soul, one aspect of the wonderfulness of myself.

He says something that at that time totally exceeds my belief system. He says that they in heaven love many things about me. I could understand that they might like one thing, but love many things? I am amazed! What could they possibly love about me?

When the other soul shoots me, I forgive him, on the spot. As the bullets are entering my body, I am thinking: "If this person has a father, he is an abusive alcoholic." I cannot believe he has ever experienced being loved, and certainly not as a child. I can only feel sorry for that other soul because he has chosen such a path.

The angel tells me that I am remembering only part of the lesson. I am remembering to forgive him, not to seek revenge, not to engage in the vendetta. I am wondering what else?

Next, in nanoseconds, St. Peter shows me fifty lifetimes I have danced with this other soul. The first lifetime is set in the time period where the humans are divided into clans.

It is dark and wintry. We are in a cave warming by a central fire. Times are very hard. I am gnawing on some piece of cooked bird. My nemesis is pulling the food away from me. He just turns around and is walking away laughing.

I remember the smooth, round stone, how it fits in my hand. I see a little Neanderthal Albert Finney jumping around, chattering about how he is mad and isn't gonna take it anymore. Red Skelton's character the Mean Little Kid says, "If I dood it, I get a whippin' . . . I dood it."

I bean the little dickens right in the back of the head. He is dead before he hits the ground. He reincarnates. He kills me. I reincarnate. I kill him. Then he reincarnates and kills me, etcetera.

The funny thing is that during the last four lifetimes, he kills me and I don't kill him. I say, "Pete, what is happening here? Gimme the skinny. What, I'm four ahead? I get to knock him off four times, gratis?"

What had happened was that I had hated him for killing me. Therefore, I had recreated him killing me. The principle is: *What you hate you recreate until you love it.* And believe me, I had more baggage stuck to me from those four lifetimes than a lot of others because I judged him for killing me.

Therefore we were "stuck" to each other. What you judge sticks to you. Remember when we were kids? "I'm rubber and you're glue. What you say bounces off me and sticks to you." We may still be stuck to some of those kids. Unless we forgive them. I don't mean just forget them. I mean love them. And that's loving ourselves as well.

When we judge people, it may or may not stick to them. It depends on whether or not they judge themselves because of our comment. Without exception, it sticks to the person who hurls the original epithet. Because no matter what the insult, it reflects perfectly some aspect of the insulter. The insult is ultimate self-judgment. Ergo, it is quite sticky.

While all this is going on, I am looking down next to me. There is a brook. I realize that there are souls in the brook, souls with whom I incarnate throughout time, my family of souls. This is my "soul stream." I find that I can be a guest in other people's soul streams.

The souls are all speaking at once. At first it sounds like babbling. Shortly, the brain catches up with the volume of input and I start to hear languages: Old English, Old French, Druid, some tonal languages I don't recognize. There are rhythms from languages, ancient, billowing out the shrouds of time. Languages no longer spoken on this planet and languages not yet spoken.

Soon it all translates into contemporary English. They are saying, "Give the kid a break, give the kid a break!" It is a magical sound, full of excitement, joy, and mystery. They are petitioning for a decision in favor of allowing my soul to return to this body.

"Peter, I truly love the soul that shot me to death. The work this soul does on my behalf is astounding. It's very labor intensive to knock somebody off fifty times."

My path includes being a murder victim because of cause and effect. I murder in a past life. The moment he shot me to death, he took the burden off my shoulders and put it on his. What a kind, noble, and loving thing to do.

He provided me with the "Shaman's Death." This is an initiation many of us choose at one point or another in life. I can clearly see the probable projection of this, my current lifetime. It looks really good. I can see even this moment of joy, as I sit here compiling this book.

I adore this other soul. I love the bullet hole in my head. It is absolute proof of my Shamanism. I complete this remembering with this other soul. I love this other soul. I love it all.

St. Peter says that while he cannot let me go into heaven at this time, he could let me have a "preview." How wonderful! Heaven trailer, what a concept! I take a step forward.

All of my life, if you asked me where my soul lived in my physical body, I would say, "In my brain, the third eye." When I step forward, I am experiencing a sensation of expanding. To my mind's great surprise, this new expanse comes from the heart, not the head.

Suddenly I am somehow an atmosphere around the planet. That is to say, I am everywhere on Earth all at once. I am listening to perhaps a billion conversations at once. Talk about a party line!

I can listen to anyone I choose, especially if my name is spoken. Same way it works down there, my name draws my attention. It seems all too confusing, all too new. I am very uncomfortable in this "new" form. Peter senses this uneasiness.

The next thing I know, I am looking down at the top of a tree. There is a bird sunning itself. I think, "Gee, a feather, that's a solar-energy collection device." A feather isn't really hollow. The energy goes in the flute, down the shaft, and into the systems of the bird. This is one hot bird I'm looking at.

No wonder birds get up when the sun comes up. No wonder they go to sleep when it goes down. No wonder they eat like birds. They're little, highly efficient, solar-energy devices. Come to think of it, as the energy enters the cortex of the bird, it experiences joy. Come to think of it, I'm the energy the bird is feeling. I'm the joy the bird is experiencing. The joy is love.

The bird is experiencing love being sunned. Being sunned equals being loved. I'm being the love the bird is experiencing. If you take anything and break it open you'll find love inside it and, come to think of it, I'm all this love! You are this love! We are all this love!

Back in the reception hall, I am told that I am a graduate. Because I remember love of this soul, whom I have danced with for eons, I don't have to return to the body. Although I have the option.

I tell him that I've paid my money and I want to continue the thrill ride called Planet Earth. I choose to return to my body, thank you. It's like the roof is suddenly ripped off the top of the cathedral.

I hear the applause of the Angelics, my ancestors, the ones I am incarnate with now, and those I will come to know. It is a thunderous ovation. Wow! Do I own! I volunteered to come here!

Peter tells me that because of universal law he is required to inform me that, due to free will, I could go down there and blow it big-time or make it even more beautiful than the dream.

As he is walking me to the door, St. Peter says, "Kid,

glad to hear you chose to get back in the game. We're gonna give ya some marbles you've never had before."

In the next scene my eyes are slowly opening. I am in a room . . . a hospital . . . monitors, the smell of disinfectant, IVs, TVs. I am radiating in that same sense of calm.

A nurse is walking by the foot of the bed. As she sees my eyes open, she makes a sharp right-angle turn in front of me. Instantly I am looking at her in the Civil War . . .

She is a nurse then also. She is stunningly beautiful, even with blood splatters on her uniform. I can smell the gunpowder. I can smell the blood. I can smell her. From the bed I see a broken Civil War soldier floating above her head.

The Civil War dimension of her looks up and begins to weep. I realize that I died in front of this soul-person in the Civil War. That broken soldier floating up there is me. I come back to life in front of her in this life. A tape loop closes in time. From this moment on I have the ability to look into other people's multidimensionality (past lives).

About a year and a half later I'm walking on a city street. I see a man, well dressed, swinging a cane as he walks. Interdimensionally I see him in a monk's robe, other monks following him. He is the one swinging the incense. I walk up to him and say, "You remember that village in Italy in the year 1358 AD?"

He looks at me, pauses for a long moment, and then slowly says, "Yes, I think I may have a past life in that area." Then I say, "Yes, you do. Do you remember some of the people, your congregation?" Again the long, slow yes. Then he asks what happens in this past life.

I tell him what I see in this brief moment: "You are so beautiful a man as you graduate the Vatican Seminary. Your first assignment is to replace a priest who has died after sixty-six years of service. You go to this village and slowly the people warm up to the 'new kid on the block.'

"Within two years it becomes the time of the plague. There are so many funerals. Always you would end the service with 'It's God's will.' Their relatives come to you and ask why God has taken this person. You only reply, 'It's God's will.'

"When 75 percent of the village is dead, the remaining 25 percent come to your home. When you answer the door someone beans you with a stone. You ask 'why?' as they stone you to death. In a Greek chorus they all say, 'It's God's will.'"

This stranger (who, it turned out, ran a metaphysical center) looks at me and says "Kid, you got a job." His words remind me so much of Peter, they give me a chill. To experience gooseflesh means you have opened up a higher dimensional access. It indicates that you resonate with this information. You have heard part of your personal truth.

One day he calls me into his office and asks me if I know why we have met this way. He says he has just realized that not once ever in his entire lifetime has he told anyone that they are the way they are because it is "God's will." Instead he tells them that if they don't like the way they are, they can do something about it. There are people at the center who will assist in their transmutation. Then he sends them to the guy upstairs doing past lives—me. I work with this man for the next seven years.

The All-Important Introduction

Every century takes all century to get around to setting the stage for the birth of the new century. It took the entire eighteenth century to herald the new form of government, democracy. It took the nineteenth to organize the flowering of the industrial revolution, which I'll simply call WWI. It has taken the twentieth to create the technological advance, the Web, which is fostering the thought evolution, the vast awakening of human consciousness, that is becoming the twenty-first century.

What will history say about the twentieth century? What is the single greatest discovery of the entire hundred years? In my opinion it is this: everything vibrates.

It is that simple. We live in a vibratory universe. Everything vibrates. I vibrate, you vibrate. Scientists have dubbed this realization the "quantum field." The quantum field is on the atomic level. The quantum field is also deep space. And it is right here, right now. Another word for "quantum field" is this room, this book—in short, *reality*.

The quantum field and everything in it, reality, is in a state of vibration at all times.

When we open our mouths and vibrate a word into the field, the vibration of the word programs the field. We tell everything what to do, all the time, with the vibrations from our words and thoughts. This is our method of programming our lives. We are born with it. This ability to tell reality what to do is God's gift to mankind. Do we know it? Do we take advantage of it?

It is the "secret." Even our slightest thoughts conduct the symphony of vibration that is the reality of our lives. This is an extremely powerful idea. It is no longer suppressed. To know this, to think this way, makes you very powerful.

The vibration of the word/thought itself is the vehicle. It carries our instruction into the field on an atomic level, on every level. We command the field by vibration of our thoughts. Words/thoughts combine our intelligence with our environment. As in, "The rose burst forth in a wondrous dance of reds and more reds." In this thought all the atoms pay attention to the choreography of reds. Another thought could make the same rose just an expensive flower that will be dead in a day or two anyway. Which thought, would you prefer?

When we vibrate any sound into existence, we link it with all other existence through the holographic principle: Everything is everything. Everything is connected to everything else. There is no separation. A fragment of one thing can describe the whole picture. Anything we say affects everything else. We direct it all.

To sum it up, we tell reality what to do every time we

open our mouths or have a thought. It is a fact. Words create reality. Thought creates reality. These are exciting new thoughts to think.

Each of us has this power, this gift, this ability. It is built in. It is switched on right now. It has been from day one. An infant has every ability to create reality with its voice. Ask any parent.

A closer examination of the idea of "words" suggests that they are predesigned, prepackaged pieces of instruction that direct the flow of our intentions. Any word is just like a software package. Our words are the programming by which we create our reality.

We use words to represent thoughts. Words are habits of thinking, not actual thinking. We often think in words, but the words are groups of decisions already made. Some of these decisions don't work very well anymore. Words are the habits of our thoughts.

The purpose of this book is to examine these habits, to render us even more fluent in our ability to program reality by choosing certain words and discarding others.

Some will say that it is our intent that counts, not the words we say. How does the universe tell the difference? The fact is, words do count and they can express our true intent, though our intent may be significantly different from our words without our realizing it.

To say "I will do this" is significantly different from "I will try to do this." They are different in intent. We are in charge of the part of the universe that manifests our reality. "Intend" is a weak word next to the word "decide."

When we are sick or embarrassed, we do not desire to talk about it. This is because speaking the words about not feeling well nail the concept into three dimensions. When fifteen people ask how we are feeling, saying that we don't feel well fifteen times begets feeling worse. It places our sacred attention on how we feel. Words do count and they count all the time. *It is a matter of where they place our attention.*

Understand that words may place our attention exactly opposite to where they were supposed to. Everyone who died on the *Titanic* was killed by the word *unsinkable*. Why? Because *unsinkable* actually means "the fear of sinking": this is where the word places the attention.

The passengers, in fact the whole world, placed their attention on one and only one outcome: unsinkable. When we exclude by saying there is only one way to be happy, we are actually placing our attention on *all other* outcomes by way of resisting them. Clearly the attention, the manifestation, was in this way placed on sinking. In other words, if the word *unsinkable* had never been uttered . . . .

Now, to get the universe to manifest our *conscious* command is the object of this book. To understand the concept of an *included* command, is a first step. An included command is where one says one thing while believing something else. For example, to say, "I will win at a poker game" while believing that one doesn't deserve the money. The universe will only hear the intent, which is the belief in undeservedness. This is because beliefs create reality, and the belief in the undeservedness exceeds, by far, the belief in winning.

Clearly then, speaking is not required to program the grid of reality. Thoughts create. To some degree, our thoughts are in word form, and thoughts, as streams of words, are subject to the prejudice of words. Therefore words also create.

This reveals the concept of preconceived ideas creating preconceived reality. Like, "algebra is hard." Hearing and believing this, one then creates the reality of algebra being hard. So if one states, "Algebra is easy," one then creates an A plus. The word *hard* creates a preconceived relationship with algebra. Algebra is not hard; it is thinking of algebra as hard that makes it that way. Put a censor on the word *hard*, never again uttering it, and life will become markedly easier. This will involve breaking the habit of, the excuse of, the way of life of "hard."

Words are tools. They are a device by which we remind ourselves and others about certain experiences. Words are not the actual experience they depict. For example, I could write one million words about diving into cool water, and the reader wouldn't be much closer to the actual experience. The thing each of us experiences is unique. So words are an approximation.

Words are not technically thought. They are at best symbols or representations of thought. Yet by their use they have enormous power, even the ability to create reality. We stream them out of our mouths constantly, usually without the slightest examination. This book is going to sharpen up that tool belt we call vocabulary!

QUADRANT

1

OBSOLETE LANGUAGE

ANY LANGUAGE, by its nature, reflects the group of beings that speak it. In a way it appears statistical. Where is the language focused? For example, there are many more words in Eskimo to describe snow than there are in English.

Language reflects the lives of the natives. We are our language—fact. Now, how does our language describe us? What is the single biggest entry in our language? How many vocabulary words are there to describe love? Not so many. For money there are a lot more. The biggest vocabulary entry may take a moment to recognize.

What is built into the fabric of our language, the easiest thing to do in it, the hallmark? Doubt. There are more ways to doubt in our language than anything else—I think, I guess, perhaps, theoretically, usually, well, sometimes, maybe, normally, often, I mean not often, don't quote me, it isn't official yet, I may be wrong but, I'll take it under advisement, I'm not sure, we'll see, maybe later, if God smiles, somehow, almost, hopefully, in the worst case, just in case, unless, what if. . . . We appear to speak a doubting language.

After a while language tends to do more than just reflect life. It perpetuates and actually creates the life of the speaker. The words we speak habitually will eventually habituate our life to their meaning. We all too easily fall into the habit of the language. A word is a decision made. In fact, all words are decisions that have already been made.

Our language cleaves in half between words of control and words of create. The one and only thing that we actually control is ourselves. The idea that we control others is an illusion. The control of someone else is done only with the complete cooperation of the other. To say we "control a situation" is to say that the situation is larger than us. When we are creating, we have accepted the situation, incorporated it inside of us, and are therefore larger than it. We can then digest it, or recreate it to our specifications.

Should vs. *Could* is a perfect example. *Should* is guilt manipulation. *Could* implies option. *Could* is open-ended potential. Words that affix us to a single outcome (control) vs. words that are holographic (create) will be revealed to us. Our choice will influence the expansion of not only our minds, but our civilization.

In the last few years a surprisingly large number of us began to edit the word *should* from speech. *Should* is, without doubt, a word that is a decision made. The decision looks like: If you do not do what you should, you are guilty. *Should* is a major guilt-manipulation word. The fact that so many of us are no longer using it indicates a major step forward.

We can do more than just stop the use of such words. We can stop "thinking in" these obsolete words. As long as we use fear-encrypted words to cause pain, we all remain less than what we could be. A way for us as humanity to stop it is for us as individuals to stop it.

As surprising as this approach may sound, it will play. The only one you have control of is yourself. The day enough of us decide to stop chattering these debilitating words, both in our heads and in our mouths, calm will just radiate to the rest of us. It is called the "hundredth monkey" effect.

Words That Disempower

All disempowering words have certain recognizable traits. They state that power and authority are outside of the individual. These words are guilt encrypted, inspiring fear; they always make us feel "less." They are designed to keep us in place, to enslave us.

There are a surprisingly large number of such words. Originally I thought of these words as short circuits in the field or dysfunctional. They function all right. They do more than just cross signals; they deaden the field at the moment they are uttered. Other words bring it to life.

Let's examine a word that is really asleep: What happens when we say "need"? Close your eyes and observe the field around you when you say this word. Just for starters, every-

need has a 2

thing takes on the signature of desperation. There is an alert. Suddenly we are climbing uphill. A subconscious program switches on, creating suffering in order to achieve getting what is needed. We are driven by lack.

But all information encoded in the word *need* is false information. There is no such thing as "need." It is a nonword. The packets of instruction contained therein are negative, sucking, antivitality. It is the nature of the word. It is a fear word. It is a slave word. Anyone who has just used the word *need* has told the entire room what they are scared to death of. They have also told everyone that they will go to any extreme to accomplish this. This is not information that is really useful to others, nor is it their business. Need is an illusion that we are outgrowing.

As we as a species evolve, we will outgrow all disempowering words and thoughts. This volume is a forerunner of the more advanced line of thought. As these ideas sprout in the fertile ground of our expanding consciousness, outdated words will take on a distinctly sour tone. Those who are not yet ready for this advance will be ever more distant from us and identifiable by their use of old fashioned language.

In the process of your transmutation, forgive yourself when these word habits slip out and just call on the higher realms to assist you in the retooling of the thought process. Human potential is truly infinite.

A List of Words That Do Not Serve Us Well

Blame: Assigning blame creates delay. This is because once we've found someone to blame, we stop the search engine;

we stop looking to ourselves for the information. It is the magician's trick of diverting attention. When our attention is placed on the one blamed, not on the resolution of the event or our role in it, cleanup can be significantly delayed. Even insurance companies have given up on blame—not because of a greater evolutionary mandate, but because it cost them time and money.

Blame drops like an anchor in your time line. Have you seen someone go into the twilight zone while they are talking about blaming someone and it's now seventeen years after the event? People get stuck in blame. To blame is to be-lame. Walk around the office saying "Assigning blame creates delay."

Block: This is the part of us we don't look at or a decision we have not made—a major clue that we left for ourselves to find. As soon as we discover it, we remember a big piece of who we really are. It also means blind spot, bump, obstacle—language that places it outside of ourselves. Tell the block to present itself in a form that is more readily recognizable.

Burden: There is a single burden, and that is guilt. Let us use the example of brushing teeth. Our parents manipulate us to brush our teeth, and then it becomes duty. Later as an adult, the manipulation, the job of "making it happen," is taken over by us. Therefore, brushing teeth becomes something we "have to do." To release the guilt is to brush because we love a clean mouth, to enjoy the experience (see Expect, p. 18).

But: It originally referred to the butting of heads, and this is exactly what the word still does. Consider the ever infamous, "I love you, BUT . . ." It takes back what was just said. It is a slam. Do you love me, yes or no?

When you hear the word "but," you've heard "I am unable to go to the new thinking." When you hear "yes, but," you've heard "I am unaware of even the concept of my inability to go to the new way of thinking." In the unconscious language it is used to refute, redirect, block. It is the last straw of denial. Once you hear it clearly, you recognize that it is always blocking you. This is good news because it means that you don't have to leave the self, to obviate the *but*.

Those of us who teach may have noticed that sarcasm doesn't serve very well as a teaching tool. The student isn't completely sure if you mean it or not. *But* is the essence of sarcasm, and sarcasm is a sibling of anger. No buts about it.

Can't: This is the poster boy of disempowered/slave thinking. As soon as you say "can't" you create impossibility. The universe must obey your every command. In order to transit out of the use of this word, understand that its purpose is to create limitation.

Of course, there are things that won't be happening at this time. This is OK. First decide to call clarity and power. Then replace the word *can't* with *won't*. This will bring clarity and power. *Won't* puts the power of decision back into your hands; *can't* takes it away and languages it as outside of yourself.

Can't is also the poster boy for the language of excuse. It is a convenient excuse when we take everything personally. "I'm not coming to the party. I can't come, because . . ."

Can't wraps any concept in the veil of unavailable. When you hear "can't," you have heard someone enact universal programming to work against something—perhaps himself. Personally I won't feel sorrow for him. Notice how different this statement is from "I can't feel sorrow for them."

Complicated: As soon as we hear "This is getting complicated," we know that there is too much brain involved. As well, we know that the heart voice has been ignored and there is enormous fear clouding the field. The universe is simplicity itself. No matter how complex it seems, there is a simple path. This path is the way toward success (see Genius, p. 72).

Conformist: Name a conformist. It isn't going to happen. Anyone we can name has, in one way or another, rocked the boat.

Criticism: Criticism depends on the ear hearing it. To really hear, hear free from ego, free from guilt, is to be inspired by criticism.

Curse: The last excuse of the superstitious mind. When we get the idea that we are cursed, we begin to build a list of things that go wrong. (There is no wrong.) We give this list of "credits" to the one doing the cursing. The more we place our attention on things going wrong, the more things go wrong. What nonsense! There is no such thing as curse.

The excuse is the refusal to take responsibility for creating our life. Remember we create 100 percent of our life, the very definition of free will.

Defeated: Defeated is the idea of having no feet. There is always somewhere to step. There is always more than one place to step (see Choice, p. 62).

Denial: Denial is a form of knowing. It is knowing divided by doubt. We can see what a large denominator doubt makes. Call denial the first stage of knowing.

Desperation: Desperation is inspiration without the joy or knowledge of our own creative potential. It is de-inspiration, it is despair of separation. (All fear is the fear of separation.) Despair occurs in the belief that separation is immutable. As usual with such a word, there is the idea that whatever is making us desperate is larger than us; simply the opposite is true.

Doubt: Doubting is another device that takes a decision away from us. Doubting is no great accomplishment. Doubt is the right hand of fear. To doubt is to break the spirit. When you hear a human being doubt, you hear their personal power drop off. The person gives up the power of their decision to things they think are unknowable. (They are highly knowable if you have the power of decision.) Build it and we will come!

We have been taught denial/doubt so well it is actually quicker than our mind. In other words, we know the answer, and then before we can blink, the denial/doubt takes over and we don't know what we just knew a moment ago. Watch it happen right in front of the mind. Think of something you know for sure. Now let's say someone asks, "Are you sure?" When you check, you are doubting, or you wouldn't have to check. You know what I mean . . . now you're not sure.

Doubt is always slightly slower than knowing. We do hear the answer, then the doubt clouds us. Sometimes this process is so quick that we "think" we don't get an answer. We do actually see the perfect answer.

Instinct is always first; logic is always second. It may be that the entire left brain is formatted as the "No" and the right brain as the "Yes" in the binary version of our human brain. When both brains are up and online, functioning as a whole, doubt is out of the equation, and neither brain is "superior."

Doubt is always about what could go awry. You could certainly go awry where there is no decision made.

Enemy: The inner-me. Have I the eyes to see the inner me? With everyone recognizing the enemy as themselves, how would war then be conducted? There is a body of evidence that says humankind has been slow on this one. However, our history is certainly not our destiny.

Before entering a relationship with one called "enemy," realize it is yourself you are confronting. Recognize the conflict as internal; resolve it and the other guy will not have to show up to do battle because there is no polar phenomenon being generated.

Evil: All evil serves divine intent. After all, without the concept evil, there would not be the idea of good. There would be no cosmos without chaos. Chaos is part of cosmos: fact.

In the land beyond right and wrong, evil is not bad; it simply is. The way the word is used today keeps us from recognizing the blessing that evil always brings.

Good/Evil is polarity thinking. To triangulate such thinking is to realize that it isn't good and evil, it just is. Thinking in this nonpolar way allows a lot more freedom of thinking and pain-free thinking. Whereas, the more we speak and think of evil as the opposite of good, the more we bind it to us. Besides, without evil there is no plot. (On other worlds evil vs. good is employed solely for entertainment.)

Expect: To expect is what we anticipate about what someone else has, or what they will do. Notice how the power is languaged outside of the self. The delightful experience of love changes at the moment our happiness is contingent upon what the other will do. This is codependence, which is a form of love. There are other forms.

Fate/Destiny: Our fate is decided by ourselves. There is no predetermined fate, otherwise there would be no free will. If we are fated to meet someone, then it is because this decision was made, in free will, prior to the incarnation. When we do meet the person, we still have the decision to make about seeing them a second time. *Everything* that happens is a decision that we make.

Destiny has a similar complexion. Our destiny is that we will evolve, that we will love. There is no predestination other than this. Again, if there were such a thing, it would be at the cost of free will. The word *destiny* means a chance up to bat. We have a chance up to bat anytime, anywhere we decide. There is no boat to miss. If there were, there would be another shortly. There is no such thing as a "once in a lifetime opportunity." Our destiny, our fate, is whatever we decide it is.

Fear: How many fears are there? Don't go making up the largest number imaginable. There is only one fear: I can't handle it if. Any thought that begins with "I can't handle it if . . ." is a fear. Every time we think we can't handle something we are losing life force. Every fear makes us grow older. There is no such thing as "I can't handle it if." That statement, that belief, is unconsciousness itself. We have handled 100 percent of it since we were conceived. Think we'll continue to handle it? Whatever it is, we're gonna deal with it, period. Key word: relax.

All fear is based on "I can't handle it if . . ." It doesn't matter what comes after this statement. It is a falsehood. Get over being afraid. It is boring. Would you watch ten thousand *I Love Lucy* episodes in a row? Of course not! Yet we will sit here and say "I can't handle it if" a hundred thousand times in a row in our thinking and not even notice. Fear is boring! Make your personal choice: freedom or another episode of "I Can't Handle It If."

What would we be thinking if it wasn't fear? What thoughts would be going through our heads? As long as we so easily fall for the bait that leads us into fear, our life, our creativity, doesn't really exist. Fear is an easy habit to break.

The first step in breaking the fear habit is recognizing it. There is one disguise that fear cannot put on. Fear cannot disguise itself from hurting you. If any thought hurts you, it is a fear thought, and you are allowed to dismiss it, as soon as it is recognized.

Once you recognize that you are having a fear, shut it off, like a light switch. Start by recognizing that you are having a fear and then snap your fingers. It's called Fear-Off. You are the one who chooses what you think.

Never mind all of the so-called "important information" in the fear; as soon as you go searching for it, you're afraid of "missing" something. Know that this information can be delivered to you by direct choice in a perfectly wonderful form. Know that if you are to adjust your flight, it will be a delight. The information contained within the fear thought" will find its way to you.

Since we have been alive we have been trained to have a very polluted and fearful thought stream. After recognizing the fear and stopping the stream of consciousness, plug your stream into the highest possible point. Snap your fingers, breaking the hold the fear has on you, then ask yourself, "What is my Highest possible thought?" You arbitrarily plug your stream of consciousness into a much higher flow. It is your birthright. Get good at this. Practice every time you have a thought that hurts you. (Highest, used in this context, is the one and only superlative in my personal languaging.)

As this Fear-Off functions, a fear will automatically transport you to your highest possible thought. This is truly limitless thinking. When we stop placing our attention on the false premise that we are helpless and tossed about by forces beyond our control, after self-love has led us to knowing that indeed we do create our lives, after we say that we will handle it *when* it happens and not before, after we arrive at the point where we see how ridiculous it is to be afraid of anything, then . . . well it's up to each individual as to what will be done with a human mind after all the ghosts have been cleared out. Where might your highest possible thought take you? What is a thought that fills you with joy right now?

All fear is myth. All fear is fiction. When we are having a fear we are not factually experiencing the event that we are afraid of. It turns out we're driving or walking or something, and actually just thinking the fear. We are automatically yanked out of the now.

Know that it is within the realm of possibility that your thoughts will never hurt you again. There are of course thousands of other clichés in our language. As you encounter them, analyze and dismiss them. Not only is it your prerogative, it is a pathway to far greater consciousness.

Frankenstein Syndrome: This is not loving one's creation. We create all of what goes on in our life. Recognizing and loving this creation is our direct movement forward. Not recognizing and loving it is movement forward, too, only indirect. Essentially, not loving everything is Frankenstein Syndrome. We fear that something we have done will turn against us. However, everything we do moves us forward. Even if something looks as if it turns against us, it's still a step in our healing.

Germs: Germs are the be-lame game, as such. As long as we have the germ to blame, we end the search. We do not look at why we created the illness. It is we who create our illness. Why create illness? It is because we live in the world of excuses. We create ourselves ill because we require an excuse to take time for ourselves. I'm not going to work! I've got a cold!

I have reclassified all germs as pets. It is a better relationship. When I become tired of playing with them, I thank them for their service and they go away.

Everything that happens in our lives is preceded by thought in higher dimensions. All illness brings a lesson to remember ("learn"). If we do not get the lesson simply by grace (in spirit), then it becomes our brain's opportunity to "get it." The mind, being unable to understand the lesson, turns it over to the body. When it is the body's turn then, physical illness is the result. The body actually has many ways to communicate with us; it's just that pain and illness are sure to be heard. If you wish to find out the spirit lesson represented by a particular disease, you may contact me by e-mail at TelepathicTV@yahoo.com.

Germs don't make you sick. You make you sick. And you make yourself well, by decision, just like everything else.

Gossip: Gossip is talking about someone when they are not present. Whether we talk lovingly or hatefully, it serves to distract us from our exchange of ideas. When someone gossips in our presence, it is to be disregarded, otherwise we are seduced into a state of judgment.

Greed: Need and greed are the same in that both have to do with satisfaction. Need recognizes only dissatisfaction. When we indulge in greed, we do not recognize when to quit. No balance point in the cycle! Both share a marked absence of gratitude. Need and greed are evil twins; even when they are called supply and demand, bull and bear. Apologies to the animals mentioned.

Hard: If we are making a decision to do something as an act of love, it is never described as hard. Our nature is to be loving. Therefore, if it is "hard," it is something that is against our nature. Since everything is love, to say "hard" is to say, we do not recognize clearly the love in the situation. Watch for this word in your thinking; it is the cue to search for a greater love, a larger picture.

Simply eliminate the word *hard*. Otherwise you manufacture a waveform designed to make the going arduous and program the situation to be much more difficult. Recognize we do this by our command. Speak the word "hard" and the universe will comply.

Replace *hard* and any words of a similar meaning with *stimulating*. It affords a positive spin and more accurately describes the situation (see Stimulating, p. 88).

Hatred: Hatred is a mirror. You see in this mirror the part of you that you don't like. As soon as you hate something you are contracted to move toward it. If this course is not modified, you will eventually become it. What one hates one recreates. In order to hate a bigot one must be bigoted. All hatred is self-hatred. Since the entire universe is designed to move toward love, when we become what we hate, we view it as self and this moves us toward love.

Headache: It is useful to remember what is going on in your mind, just before your headache is first noticed. In order to understand the principle behind headaches we must understand that we human beings are *love generators*. A headache means that something is blocking this flow of love. We have withheld our love from something. If we call someone a "headache," we are withholding our love from this person.

When we withhold love, love redoubles its effort to get out of us; we feel the blood pressure growing in the *cabeza*. Find something to love about the individual, the situation, the thought, because it is really only yourself that you are withholding love from. Create love, give love. This is what we do. Do this, or continue on the headache construct.

Heathen: Anyone who believes in a point of view that is not your point of view. There are more heathens than ever before, so wiping them out doesn't work. The response is to celebrate diversity.

Hope: This is a trick word designed to get us to give up our power of decision. If we hope for something, we are not deciding the something. In other words, when we just decide something, there is no doubt, and therefore there is no use for the word *hope*.

When we desire something, yet do not decide it, we "hope" for it. It enters reality on a default code. As long as we hope for anything, we doubt it. Decide instead. To say "hope" out loud is to abandon the sovereignty of the creation of life.

The concept of having no hope is like a double default code decision. In other words, you are no longer doubting how hopeless (itself a form of doubt) things are. Yet we still keep watch, thus injecting a third doubt code, entitled "just in case," / "hoping against hope." Notice how we never hope with hope. This would be a negative-positive-negative code. Dismiss all these little tangles as being nonsense. Decide, don't hope. In fact, boast of being "hopeless."

Idealist: An idealist is someone who believes that yin can exist without yang. The concept that cosmos can exist without chaos is naive, as they define each other. Together they are the whole. Idealism is another ism that drives us.

If, or, the Myth of If: *If* was originally coined to assist us to explore options. If this, then that. However with everyone languaging everything as outside of themselves, saying "if" leaks our power, specifically, the power of decision.

Often the word *if* is used in place of a decision. As in, "If it rains, I won't go to the picnic." You decide "if" it is going to rain—or pretend that you aren't deciding. Listen for the word "if" in speech.

If you don't believe me, I understand this. I do not make your decisions for you. The free will of another person makes it impossible to dictate the other's behavior. "If" is therefore inherent in the respect of another's free will. The only place in speech where we use the "if" word is when it has to do with someone else's choice. Otherwise it indicates a decision is hidden behind a veil. Even then, we still create 100 percent of our life, so "if" becomes marginal. Under any circumstance, using it results in a loss of decision/distinction.

One of the big clichés is "what if." It is more than a cliché, it is a way of life, or more accurately, a way of thought. Even more accurately, it is a way of doubt! How foolish we may feel to remember that "what if" is a default decision. We are being tricked into giving up our sovereign power of decision to smoke and shadow.

In other words, "what if" keeps us from making the decision. The word *if* means something doesn't exist yet. Will it exist at all? However, its existence is determined by our decision. These "if" situations automatically don't exist unless we decide they exist. The situation is given life by our decision. It may not appear this way (smoke and mirror), yet it is our decision.

To sum up, whenever you hear "if," it means make a decision then and there, period.

Impressed: We can successfully admire someone for their modeling and still realize our own light at the same time. This is something that is growing within us.

If you feel impressed, connect it to a trigger that automatically keeps this from being the comparison game and therefore a loss of your own personal light (repression).

Insanity: This is a label that dehumanizes a person. It separates. The insane bear no responsibility. Anyone who is considered insane is just a person who is having great fear.

We were all raised by controlling limitation. When we are afraid, we desire to be controlled. As the conscious channel Carla Neff Gordon said on Telepathic TV, "Insanity is where one goes when one does not feel safe." The first thing to do when playing with someone who is pretending to be insane is to allow him or her to feel safe.

Inspect: Technically, to inspect is to look within. So it is not the contents of the package that we inspect, but our relationship with the contents. If there appears to be something missing, it is more within the self than the package. Knowing that we are whole within ourselves suspends the concept of "disappointment," until the "missing" stuff can arrive.

Insult: An insult is a distortion of opinion. When we insult, we are expressing what we do not love about ourselves! This concept is rarely known. The information someone gives us, when they insult us, is exactly what they don't like about themselves.

This information is a razor-sharp sword. Freely behead insulters. To not do this is to invite a further tangle. When someone says, "You look funny," we may say, "We're all mirrors for each other" (replacing "Have you looked in a mirror lately?").

Remember, we know when not to speak. We say nothing when anything that we say would be used against us.

Issues: Let me finally put to rest the issue of issues: To describe something as an issue suggests inherent opposition. The situation has already turned to stone. To have an issue is to break from a state of divine being. It results in our placing our sacred attention on discord. I quote/para-phrase Eleanor Roosevelt:

> "Great minds discuss ideas.
> Average minds discuss events.
> Small minds discuss people."
> Politicians discuss issues.
> What more is there to say?

Judgment: Judgment is really prejudgment. When we are judgmental, we have already decided something is right or wrong. It has very little to do with opinion. The principle that is functioning is a decision to make something wrong, or for that matter, to make something right. When we judge something, we make it wrong or right. When we leave this paradigm, things are neither right nor wrong; they simply are.

Learn: In our God consciousness we remember that we have come here with all knowledge. It is just a matter of remembering. The thing about the word *learn* is that it always requires effort. It's the epitome of movement forward by abuse. As in, "Haven't you learned this yet?"

We cannot learn anything until it is remembered. There are more ways to remember than by learning. Much more effortless, much vaster, spontaneous remembering is available to anyone upon request. We have all known something spontaneously, there just has never been a way to own the expression of this talent.

Learn is the middle man of education.

Luck: This is the quintessential expression of "My power lies outside of me." Once I went about six months unable to get an answer to a particular question. I finally gave in and as I was reaching for a tarot deck I heard a voice say that the reason that I couldn't get the answer was that I hadn't decided yet. Instantly, I realized that if I decided one outcome, I'd draw the ace of abc, and if I decided a different outcome, I'd draw the deuce of xyz. There is no such thing as luck, there is only decision. Whether this is a conscious decision or an unconscious decision is on the watch of each of us.

Meat: After the last nuclear winter, when mankind was about to leave the face of the earth, antelope jumped into the circle of elders and declared (pardon the expression) "eat me." This soon heralded the motto "me eat." Which of course was shortened to simply "meat."

In the trilogy of body, mind, and spirit that we all inhabit, it is exciting to assist the physical body in raising its vibration. The body can be a true ally in our advancement. However, with the body contributing a substantially lower frequency for its third of our trinity, there are heights that are simply not reached through it. And there are certain things that a person who eats meat isn't gonna get. One of them is: there are certain things a carnivore isn't gonna get.

The feeling of the body being truly light must be felt first hand. Running on a lighter diet, possibly a diet of all living foods is far more readily available than it may at first appear.

Mystery: There is no mystery at all as soon as we know that the universe exists to please us. In our backward training we tell the universe to look like a mystery. The universe accommodates. We tell the universe that we are not good at manifesting and the universe accommodates us, every time. What would happen if we told the universe that we understand it? There is no mystery.

Need: A holy man in India had himself buried alive for two weeks. When he was dug up, he didn't even take a deep breath. This event is famous; it repeats on television. How did he do it? He funded his body directly from the universe. He did not even "need" oxygen. Such knowledge is not yet common knowledge; however, it will be. Perhaps if you or I ran out of oxygen, in moments we would be at a much higher frequency. I assure you we would be very happy about it.

We do not need anything. *Need* is a non-word. There is no such thing. It is just a habit, an addiction, a useless and hurtful self-indulgence. It is a word used by dark advertising wizards to trick people into buying useless junk. Whatever it describes moves away from you.

Does the universe contain all of everything? Yes. Then how is need possible? Need exists only in the sleepy-slave realities. The word is one of the major sour notes in the symphony that is the vibration of our reality. Understand that this word tricks us into placing our creativity (our precious attention) on not having something. How stupid is this?

Have you ever described a person as "needy"? Fearful, weren't they? It is a word designed to strike terror/guilt manipulation response. Every time you use that word, *you* are that needy person.

We may be unconscious of the number of times in a day that we use the word *need*. Totally remove the word from speech; relax, and stop needing. Think about it; if you never again use the word *need* you will, therefore, automatically never be needy again. It is easier to stop using the word than to continue using it. Stop using it and it stops the thought form. Decide, create the ability to stop using the word *need*. Suggested replacement words: select, choose, create, make, attract, desire, wish, convene, *love*!

Obsession: Obsession is passion without reason. Each of us has a little voice within us called the "voice of reason." The concept is to hear and listen to this voice. For example, when we are obsessive we may work beyond our point of exhaustion, never once hearing our inner voice telling us to rest.

There is a myth that champions push themselves beyond their limit. This is not true; champs pushes themselves *to* their limit. In this way, the next time, the limit extends.

Original sin: Doesn't it bother you how innocent newborn babies are? Well, it did distinctly bother some early church people. So much so that in A.D. 256 a college of cardinals was convened. They invented original sin. The beloved mother of mankind became the be-lamed Eve.

These early pontiffs (pontificators), pretending to see evil everywhere, tagged us as quickly as possible. "Get 'em right from the start" (as translated from the original Latin). Let's just call it what it is, "original guilt." The sooner we can be convinced we are evil and therefore guilty, the sooner we can be neatly folded into the flock, enlisted in the workforce. When we think we are guilty, we are controlled.

Congratulations! You can now toss "Original Guilt." We are not guilty, and we do not have to continue to act guilty. To no longer think of yourself as somehow guilty is freedom. It is not a state of doing, it is a state of being. Be free. It is new and unusual. You are not guilty of being not guilty! Act like it.

Panic attack: Remember that you are the one who chooses what's in your head. This is a truth, an absolute. From moment to moment, you are the one who makes the choice of happy or sad. You can indulge yourself to think otherwise, but it is true. We refer to it as free will.

Thoughts that do not serve you are easily dismissed. Someone may think, "I don't know how easily those thoughts could be dismissed," and they would be correct: they don't know. Undesired thoughts are quite easy to dismiss. "Be in pain or dismiss the thought"; it is always down to this, and it is much easier to stop the thought than to "think" yourself in writhing agony.

It is more than just dismissing the fictional fears. Give your mind a path to lead you to your greater potential. Say, "All right, none of this panic is real; what is the greatest possible joy of thought I can experience instead?"

Pharmacy: (inside vs. outside) The "p" in pharmacy is silent; it's pronounced "harmacy." The human body is the most sophisticated pharmaceutical laboratory in the universe. What's more, you're the boss of it. Tell your body that you are done playing with your new pet (the illness), thank it for all the fun, and say good-bye. The body will then play with chemistry. Chemistry is, after all, the body's forte. We command and, voila, we become vital again.

Our conscious, living Mother Earth is invested in our well-being. Anything that can go off balance (illness) can be rebalanced by a plant sticking right out of her surface. There is no question of this. The object is to find this plant and *process it as little as possible*. Then consume it as naturally as possible. There are backup plants for every plant there is, so do not think of the diminishing rainforest as loss in this regard.

If a plant appears unavailable, tell the body to manufacture the enzyme, nutrient, or other substance and to return to a robust state of being. Our immune system when even moderately online is magnificent to behold! It's our diet that is clogging us up. Go to *www.curezone.com* for more information.

Prayer: The word *prayer* assumes and affirms that we are separate from God. Actually, prayer is any thought, in anyone's head, at any time. The reason that God knows every thought in your head is that you are God. No matter what we do, we touch the universe. When we to wish to put something in God's in basket, we make a decision (see Decision, p. 64).

Problem: Again this is a word that has changed over time. Originally it was pronounced "probable-blame" (see Blame, p. 12). When we spend a life solving problems, we are human doings, not human beings. Let us boldly take the power of our words and replace the word *problem* with *symptom*. Then we begin to look at the truth of the situation. "Houston, we have a symptom."

Hearing of a "problem," we armor up. We begin to create under the false premise that the solution must be difficult, hard, painstaking. Painstaking—who thinks up these words? Never mind, you would describe it as a "difficult problem." These two words used together have been known to be fatal.

Our problem is really a symptom of something. And that something is within our own personal belief system. Like the problem of no money is a symptom of low self-esteem. We do well to view the internal factors as key. Eventually we may automatically replace the thought "problem" with the concept "opportunity," now that's languaging. "Houston we have an opportunity."

Program: Programming is being told what to think, how to react. It is an element of what Deepak Chopra calls "precognitive commitment." This is the idea that we see what we believe, not what is there. This is the nature of programming.

Recognizing how we have been programmed and replacing it with upgraded material is the reason for this entry. We are programmed to believe certain "realities." Believing is not so much seeing as it is selecting. Programming equals paradigm perimeters. It's synonymous with education.

Remember Pavlov's dogs. The dogs salivated every time the bell rang because they had been programmed for bell = food. It used to be that every time my phone would ring, I'd armor to deal with someone, something. I wrote "Pavlov" on the back of the phone to remind me to choose what the call is. This is programming to re-write existing programming. Call programming to awaken you; call it into your life right now. Write "Pavlov" on your phone in large letters.

Psychotic episode: Psychotic episodes occur when we are in great fear. We feel that we will not be heard, believed, capable of something. This phenomenon involves brain space.

In our society, we are not taught how to delete things that do not serve us. If someone is insulted, a tape loop of the insult starts going on in the person's head, playing over and over again. This takes up a lot of brain space, and consequently there isn't much left to do normal thinking. You may have seen people given such shocking news that they couldn't remain standing. This is because they didn't have the room in the brain to process the news and maintain standing.

Let's say that we are in a car and we tell the driver to make a left, and they wax psychotic on us. We were not in error; the driver just did not have enough brain space available to drive the car, have the conversation, watch traffic, and suddenly factor in making the left while processing who knows how many open tape loops. So the individual has to take most of this off-line in order to get the brain space necessary to make the turn.

From the outside, the shutting down of all these systems looks like a psychotic episode. When the new brain boots up, the focus is on the turn. This requires less bit drive and so the turn is made. Still, it wasn't the turn that took up the remaining brain space so much as the fear of making the turn. As we delete fear from our lives we automatically have more brain space.

Reality: Does reality create belief? Does belief create reality? From a scientific viewpoint, the basic premise is that reality is a constant and it is to be studied. A different view is that we study our beliefs to create reality. In this world one must believe it to see it. This may be why science remains skeptical (see Skeptic, p. 40).

Right and wrong: Two words designed to keep us in the box all right! We introduce in this book the idea that anything that looks bad or wrong is really a very condensed good. It may take years to see why a particular "bad" event has its blessings. Nonetheless, every event does have a blessing.

We are almost never taught this concept. As long as we remain trapped in the unending battle between "good and bad" we are trapped in perpetual "re-action." We are constantly attacking bad and defending good. Good and bad will take up all of our brain space and all of our time, our entire life.

Right and wrong are abusive words of limitation. We can discard their use. Instead, think differently. Think in the terms "this serves me" or "this does not serve me." This is nonjudgmental, and your opinion is served. Preference is a natural state of being.

Request a spirit guide named Rumi. He was incarnate as a Sufi poet in Turkey. Ask him to guide you to the Land Beyond Right and Wrong.

Every few days, I used to walk by a stand of pines that had been there for about fifty years. One day they were all cut down. This was a great shock to me. For a while, I could only think of what a loss, a setback it seemed. Animals homeless, air no longer scented with the wonderfulness of pine. I suffered greatly for this.

Finally my emergency angel came to me to say that the Earth herself was OK with it. The trees themselves agreed to it as well. The animals had already found new abodes. The man who cut them down did it to feed his family. Even I agreed to it, so that I could recognize the entrance to the land beyond right and wrong. I began to relanguage.

The trees being cut down is certainly not right. It is certainly not wrong. It simply is. The freedom is astounding. Peace is in the eye of the beholder. Begin to build the place in your mind marked the Land Beyond Right and Wrong. And as Rumi says, "I'll meet you there."

The fictional battle between right and wrong is like the conflict between knowing and doubt. Knowing and doubting are the same thing (states of mind); it's just that doubt makes it take much longer to get anywhere. Choose the path of good and bad, and at the end of your life there will still be just as much good and bad. Make a different choice.

Sacred space/Comfort zone: First of all, the comfort zone is not the fort you build around your sacred space to keep people and information out. It's the one you build to keep yourself out.

The term *sacred space* is a misnomer because it implies separateness. It is impossible not to be in your sacred space. You are in your sacred space, period. You have your integrity, your borders, all that is sacred to you within you. How could your sacred space be outside of yourself? This idea is typical of the mythos rampant on this planet. Are you sacred, yes or no?

Your comfort zone is exactly the perimeter of your belief system. Are you comfortable in the presence of aliens? Your belief system creates your reality. Like everything else, your belief system will evolve (adapt).

Anywhere that I step is holy ground.

Sadness: Author Mary Phelan says, "Sadness is love acted out in a paradigm of separation." One does not have to create in a paradigm of separation. We are not separate. All of the ones who have passed over are not separate from us; they are just in another dimension. Placing the sacred human attention on separation is not a choice that serves.

Sadness can be habit forming. All addiction is a search for happiness divided by guilt. There are dozens of ways to identify yourself as guilty in any event that appears to generate sadness. This is just the way we have been taught to think. After a while, holding on to this masochism is unsightly. It does not serve us. We are not guilty. Yes, one could have done something differently, so what (see Guilt, p. 106)?

Sadness is a fear. It is a fear about being incomplete. Radiate in the knowledge that you are complete at all times (whole).

Scientific method: We now realize that scientific experiments are directly, substantially affected by the expectations of the person doing the experiment.

Secret: The words means "it must be revealed." Probably at the most inopportune moment or the most humorous moment, which are always synchronous. *Secrecy* may be defined as fear of knowing.

There are no secrets. Withholding the flow of knowledge is an impossibility. The idea of withholding the flow of knowledge is inherent in what we call "intellectual property."

Assumed possession of ideas as some form of property is, let's say, a fallible concept. Someone manufactures little square crackers. Someone else desires to manufacture little square crackers. You cannot own the idea; you cannot really own the crackers. Eventually we will have a world without money, where everyone does exactly what they would love to do and trusts that it's all OK.

Do I somehow own the thoughts in this book? And do you, therefore, require license from me to think in the ways suggested herein? No. This volume is in no way my intellectual property. I do not own its knowledge. Once knowledge becomes sealed off it dies from the lack of flow. Witness every secret society ever in history.

Here is how it goes. Let's say I buy a seed from someone. I plant it and water it and there is fruit produced. Guess who owns the fruit. Even though the seed knew the DNA codes. This book is a sacred seed usufruct!

We do not take a secret to the grave. It takes us. All of this is not to say that there is nothing that is private. The word *secret* states that information is withheld in order to manipulate. Privacy is something that we all have a right to. Each of us is allowed to have things that are for us and us alone. Private doesn't mean hidden. Privacy is a birthright. To experience privacy, it will be necessary to exhibit borders. Borders are self-love in action. There is a major difference between borders and resistance.

Separation: How possible is this? All fear is based on the fear of separation. We are never actually separate; we are in a state of being afraid of being separate. No matter what, we are still a part of all that is.

All right, let's say you're alone. Who are you telling that you are alone? If you can actually be alone, call Guinness.

Shame: More easily recognized in its original hyphenated form, sham-me. We have "shame" cattle-prodded into us from the beginning. Want to lose a big piece of the box? Actually forget how to be ashamed of yourself or anyone. Be unabashed in the pursuit of bliss.

Skeptic: Name history's greatest skeptics. Time's up. It's a trick question. There is no such thing as a great skeptic. To doubt is no accomplishment whatsoever. Who hung out in the bar with Orville and Wilber and told them, "Ah, no, you'll never get something heavier than air to fly." What was the name of the judge who sentenced Galileo? See? History forgets the names of the skeptics and remembers the idea. This is because the idea has a greater resonance.

Skeptics have no power unless someone is attempting to convince them of something. Skeptics can never actually be convinced. We attempt to convince them; they just find more doubt. It is their job to convince themselves; it is not our job.

A skeptic will go down on one word. This word is *trick*. They never stop looking for the trick. Ask a skeptic what he holds as an unshakable belief. If he has one. Whatever it is, tell him that it turned out to be a trick. Stand back.

Curiosity is a function of the left brain. Skepticism is a distortion of curiosity. It is the right brain, in conjunction with the whole brain, that has the ability to know. Skeptics never know anything. Skeptics think with half a brain.

Actually they have recently isolated the gene that makes a person skeptical, but no one will believe them.

Slavery: Lincoln was referred to as "the great emancipator." He did his work a century and a half ago. Yet our language freely refers to ownership of humans. My employee, my spouse, my child, my boss, my teacher, my waitperson. Get it? There, that's my reader. What nonsense. You are your own reader.

The origin of all forms of slavery is desire. Spoken as "do-sire," we remove the delay that makes for enslavement. In other dimensions manifestation is instant and there is no slavery.

Another way to arrive at freedom is to enter a state of desirelessness. One may indeed renounce the path of materialism. Yet another option is to use the technique of detaching from a single outcome (see "Words of Attachment to a Single Outcome," p. 103). Bless it if it does; bless it if it does not, now choose.

Spend: This is a word ending in the letter *d*. It will never be in present tense. It's gone, it wasn't ever really fully in the now. We can replace the concept of spending more with the idea of spinning. "It's all in the risk." See how easily our language evolves?

Stress: Stress is the fear of being disapproved of by someone. Stress is another word for guilt, and it drives our society. If you cannot find someone to disapprove of you, you'll disapprove of yourself. (This is where stress becomes ridiculous.)

This process of stress is easily dismissed. We are all doing as well as we can all the time. No matter what, we are at peak performance, all the time, for that particular time. When asleep, we're at peak performance being asleep. When we wake up slowly, we wake up slowly at peak performance. We are our nature. If someone disapproves of this, so what? It is just them disapproving of their own nature.

Struggle: Do you prefer to struggle with or to struggle against? Struggle is self-tugging. This is another word coined in the lack of commitment to the self. When we struggle, we don't decide; we don't command; we tug.

The very concept of struggle suggests that the solution is outside of your ability to create. It isn't. Don't struggle, just be. Nothing can get a grip if you don't resist. Place the sacred attention on where you would prefer to be, not on how "difficult" getting there is. Write the affirmation "I no longer have to struggle with my own mind." This will automatically result in moving toward clarity, the very clarity that the word *struggle* belies.

Suspect: This is another form of doubt. (The purpose of this book is to eliminate the majority of doubt in thinking.) Suspicion exists, like a wedge, between knowing and action. When we stop suspecting, we must know. Knowing can be done without a body of evidence. Knowing is an attribute of higher mind.

Taboo: This is a word that commands you to do. Yet you know that in doing so there's risk. What a bind for a word to put us in. It speaks to the true dysfunction of the world of "control." *Taboo,* a word designed to inspire fear, means something that is joyous to do. Take the boo out of your taboo. Do not boohoo me your taboo. Indeed do (see Obedience, p. 81).

Temper: Yet another word that underlines how little self-creation we appear to have. *Temper* is a word designed of reaction, a word of excuse. "That's quite a temper" doesn't excuse very much. Both *temp* and *per* show the fleetingness of temper. When we are angry, we don't have all the information. This is what's temporary, what's fleeting. When temper flares, out of self-love, don't speak. In a few moments the info will come and there will have been no reason to be angry. This is the essence of the idea of counting to ten to banish anger. Those who use this counting technique are, overall, less embarrassed (see "The Dialect of the Bully," p. 140).

Temptation: This is a word of manipulation; thinking with it automatically reduces desire and inspiration to guilt. Think more in terms of creation. The word *temptation* actually takes the fun *out* of things. Guilt goes in; fun goes out. Remember, temptation is inherently temporary.

Try: Another very popular slave word. Obviously there is the implication of effort. The "I will" part of the word. What is this will focused on? Answer: doubt. Another way to say it is "indecision." So *try* means "I will focus effort on no decision. I place my attention on doubt." Is this the classical definition of insanity? Effort that is focused on no decision . . . What?

Trying and commitment are mutually exclusive. Don't use the word *try* if you desire credibility. When people say they're going to try to be at the party, I say I'll try to set a place. Replace *try* with *explore*, which is a word that has enough coding to reset the circuit.

Upset: To hear this one a little more clearly, it means that one has been "set up." Guess who did the set up!

Want: The slave word that is used to create separation. As soon as our voice creates "the want" waveform, want is created. When we say we want something, we are declaring it to be apart from us. It is synonymous with the word *need*. Have you ever used the adjective *wanton* to describe someone? Were they not indeed needy? Replace *want* with *create* or *attract* and watch magic enter your life.

Weapon: Weep on.

Whine: The accent that fear gives your voice. No one likes the squeaky wheel. Whine, and you tell everyone in the room that your parents rewarded you for whining. Of course, that same policy is in place as far as your children's upbringing. Most, but not all, of the dialect of Victimese is spoken with the whine accent (see "The Dialect of Victimese," p. 120).

Work/Play: *Work* is a four-letter word, all right. So is *play*. The first is a slave word; the second is a word of power. They both refer to life.

When we work, what we are doing is against our nature—it is spiritless participation done out of duty, obligation, and guilt. The motivation is to get paid, not have fun. Play is elation, joy, and fulfillment. Since we all know that we can love a job and therefore turn work into play, let us stop using the word *work*. Work is self-imposed servitude (the work is the master). Play is where the player is the master. Think of this the next time you play a game of "chance."

The line "put away the things of childhood" has killed many an inner child. Breathe life into your personal inner child. This breath technique will "work"—I mean play.

Cliché Removal

The majority of clichés in our language are like little dark holes sucking life from all around it. They catch on only because they sound clever. I have never heard a clever cliché. We could make some up. "Don't you just hate it when . . ." could be changed to "Don't you just *love* it when." It's a completely different reality. Move in.

A cliché is just a larger chunk of verbal instruction stirred into the soup that is language. We are going to add some new ingredients and begin the recognition of useful versus useless information. "It's just an expression" usually means that it is just a repression.

The following list will aid in recognition, analysis, and dismissal of these expressions. This includes the effect it will have on our subconscious and therefore on our life. These ideas, which find their way into our mythos by being repeated again and again don't do anything other than keep us asleep. They are unusually deeply ingrained. "Wouldn't ya know."

"Can't teach an old dog new tricks.": Our education is more than just a lifetime progression. Our growth, our evolution never stops. The older we are, the more experienced, the more aware, the better we become. Once we remember not to stuff our heads with inconsequential chatter, once we remember how to think effectively, things like Alzheimer's won't be occurring. Mary Phelan, author of *The Teacher Within,* points out that it is we who create our DNA, not our DNA creating us. What power!

"Can't tell a book by its cover.": This fuels the paradigm of mistrust. It is an insult to the fine sensory and extrasensory array that we all have. It is an epithet of disenfranchisement. It is used as excuse.

First clue: the slave word *can't*. This cliché lives in the world created in the doubt of our own knowing. If we were more connected to nature and our nature, the expression might be "You can tell a tree by its bark" (see Trust, p. 89).

"Good for you"; "Builds character"; "No pain, no gain": Epithets of the martyr. We can grow, evolve, and change without the cattle prod of pain. These expressions are the rationalization of "failure." There are no failures; there is just more information. Live pain free; live knowing of our greatness.

"I knew it.": At the moment one "knew" it one must have been picturing it. However, knowing is not just picturing it, but also deciding it. In this phrase, our power is so disconnected from our consciousness that it's only in the future that we "knew" it. "I knew it" actually means "I doubted it."

Our ability to picture possible futures is aligned with our power to create these futures. Once we understand this we can easily cancel something we may not care to create (see Cancel, p. 61).

"I'll get it done somehow.": Martyrdom much? This is the masochistic method of living up to some small percent of our human potential. We do command the universe. The "somehow" is the universe coming to assist us. It suggests that the mind is (not yet) able to perceive its own power. Instead: I'll get it done in my own timing. I will create it masterfully. Chill. It will be done.

"I'm confused.": Search first and foremost for the answers inside. Confusion and guilt are at first indistinguishable. The decision "I'm confused" is preceded by a feeling of lack, commonly known as guilt.

"I told you so.": Oddly this is the statement that means someone has gotten someone else to create in their reality.

47

Someone predicts a disaster, and someone else hears this and then creates it. Is this cliché an admonishment or a boast? Either way, it simply isn't interesting. In our society we are realizing that validation is internal. Seek your own internal validation.

"I told you so" says that the speaker is seeking validation, recognition of their knowing, their ego, their will over yours. To the "I told you so," one may reply, "Thank you. And yet I still trust my own instinct."

"Just in case.": When we decide something, it is activated. To doubt it by making alternate choices "just in case" voids the original decision. Decide and let it go through. "Just in case" is the habit of self-doubt (see If, p. 25).

"Just our luck.": The affirmation of resignation. The word *luck* is listed in the first section as a slave word (see Luck, p. 28). In general our language is superstitious. It is full of words and expressions that give up our power to external circumstances that (we are told) are against us. Nothing about this expression is true. Make decisions, not resignations.

"Off the wall.": Walls represent the boundaries of one's belief systems. If someone says you are "off the wall," they mean that you have somehow exceeded their belief system. You are "beyond the walls" of this individual's comfortable reality. Congratulations are in order. You have helped another expand the borders of their thoughts.

"Part of me . . .": When you say a part of you feels something, you are not united. You are issuing conflicting commands, divided decisions. Nothing will manifest. Unite! Decide which is the greater part and render self-sovereignty.

"Play it safe.": Playing it safe is actually not playing at all because everything is safe to begin with. To be in pain or believe that we are hurt involves forgetting who we really are. In order to actually play, in order to experience love, we must be willing to risk. We risk experiencing the illusion of not being loved. Well, as I said, it is all safe to begin with.

"That's not so funny.": It really means "That's not so healed."

"The only fear is fear itself.": It is possible to live a life of fearlessness.

"Too good to be true.": This is the command to stop enjoying and return to our normal not so good. It is yet another epithet of the martyr. It is the result of being brought up in polarity thinking. (As soon as we figure out where we are, we immediately seek to go to the opposite place.) The first clue is the superlative, "too."

This expression could be understood as guilt manipulation: "Too good to be true for me." Little guilt tags like "for me" exist right below the surface throughout the language. It is the basic sense of unworthiness we were programmed with.

The expression also implies a quid pro quo relationship between good and bad. No such relationship actually exists.

"Too many cooks spoil the soup.": This may or may not be true. What I do know is that this is an easy way to dismiss another's authority. And let's not forget that it's up to others whether or not their authority is dismissed.

"What can I do?": Assist humankind to advance, make the world a better place. It is done in a very simple way. Each of us works on him- or herself. Then the big picture transmutes. What I can do is be a better me.

"What goes up must come down.": This is the reason that success may seem so fleeting. With our own voices we keep a successful process from continuing to work.

"What goes up must come down." Not if it achieves escape velocity. Reply with, "Things are getting better and better."

"Why is it always me?": This cliché may look like a question, a complaint, yet it is a decision. Actually it is a command. Enter a different command.

"Worst-case scenario": Exactly how many times has the worst case actually happened? And was anyone actually effectively prepared? Why would anyone consider such a thing? If rational thinking is the only tool used, there won't be enough brain space to list all the variables. The worst case is not possible to know.

If "worst case" comes up in conversation, just say, "Before we discuss the worst case, let us decide the future, instead of giving our power up to some superlative with a persecution complex." (*Worst* being the superlative and the general negativity of the statement being someone's persecution.) Write on a piece of paper: I no longer think of my self as persecuted. Worst-case scenario or we decide the future—pick one.

"You never get another chance to make a first impression.": Exactly how much of my power am I to give up to the fear of being disliked? This cliché is a demeaning fear manipulation that suggests being yourself is somehow incorrect, if not dangerous.

Don't forget that it is likely a friend has told you this. They may or may not be aware of what a disparaging effect this may have on your self-confidence. All you have to do is act naturally. Ringo Starr told this to the world in the 1960s. You heard him.

Changing Our Speech

The habit of thought and therefore speech may transform by the study of this text. As these words that don't serve us well occasionally slip out in everyday conversation, forgive yourself, be kind to yourself. Every time it happens, cancel and then say, "I call to me the higher languages."

The words that do not serve us well may sound as sour notes to our ears when spoken in our presence. Others may in their love for us wish to speak without these words. Each of us must change for ourselves before any true revision can be made in the thought process of our race. We serve ourselves well in patience, gently, yet relentlessly, reminding ourselves and others of the great potential in our language, always avoiding the harsh tones.

QUADRANT

2

WORDS AS POWER

THE BELOVED CHRONICLE of the Bible informs us that in the beginning there was the "Word." When God spoke the Word, all of creation came into being. (No one seems to know what the exact word was, but it's probably just as well, because were it spoken again, everything in the world would double.)

God gives this "power of the word" to us, his children. It is our birthright. Any word we speak has this "creation" effect on the everything. We have a Godlike sovereignty over our life. Whenever we speak a word (any word), it tells the universe exactly how to act. This gives us the grand satisfaction of being able to steer the universe anytime we make (speak/think) a choice. It is our decision that tells everything how to act. This is the activation code for the all that is. We could look at this as "managing" the universe for God.

Any time that we speak our choice, we speak in words of power. It cannot be done any other way. What puts the power in our speech is the *knowing* behind the words. When we know, doubt no longer robs us of power.

All words are words of power because the universe responds to any vibration we humans make. In the first part of this book we looked at certain words that we are better off not speaking, slave words that have the power of "controlling" us. To not utter these words of disempowerment is to automatically speak more powerfully.

In this section we are discussing words of power. What these words have in common is that they bring us more in line with our true nature. They are a joy to speak. They are in and of themselves fun generating. Inherently they add effervescence into the currents of life.

Which words give you pleasure to speak? Search your data banks. Make a list of words that feel good to you and speak them more often. You will automatically be a more powerful person. Stop and think about the real message in each word—spoken or thought. Look through our language; the words discussed in this book are just some broad strokes. Your thoughts, your speech are your activator system; it's up to you what you activate. Live life with the word *magnificent* turned way UP LOUD!

Vocabulary Equals Power

Native intelligence—the ability to solve, to evolve—is not vocabulary dependent. Joy may be found in abundance with no words whatsoever. Nonetheless, words are fundamental building blocks of thought, and therefore of our life. The more words we have a true command of, the greater the scope of understanding, the greater the knowing, the greater the authority, the greater the capacity.

With this in mind, then, let's explore some vocabulary that can add power to your languaging. Many are words you already know but perhaps don't use or don't use to powerful effect. Words of power are not spoken, they are freed. When joy is the byproduct of our speech, we are reaching the new plateau.

A List of Words That Serve Us Well

Abundance: It's internal not external. It is like a tide; it goes in and out, but within that range, there is all that is required. More abundance, less abundance—these are games fools play. Abundance is a state of being, not doing. There simply is abundance. All abundance is total abundance. One *is* abundance, one does not *have* abundance.

Acceptance: To accept is to make ourselves larger, to include that which we would resist as part of us and then to change it. Once something is accepted, there is no resistance, and then we can dissipate it. With resistance, we are tricked into placing the sacred attention on that which is resisted and therefore grow it larger. In accepting, we cast ourselves in the role of creator instead of controller.

Act: This word is to replace "re-act." It is this author's opinion that about three thousand years ago, one of us acted

57

and the rest of us have been re-acting ever since. To stop re-acting and begin acting is to have an original thought. "Acting guilty" is more accurately spoken as "Re-acting guilty." Act is a very powerful concept for us. Act changes thinking into being.

Angeling: Allowing others to help. Angels stand by awaiting our request for assistance. Angels are the part of the universe that one has to ask for in order for it to activate. It is no different than asking your arm to move.

When we ask our arm to move we are acting within the part of the universe that is our body. When we ask the angels to activate, we are acting within the part of the universe that is the rest of us. It is still part of us; it just looks like it is outside. Gratitude is experienced on both sides. Don't forget that Angelic resources are inexhaustible.

Annanda: *Annanda* is a Hindi word that means perpetual bliss. Here is how to actually live in this state. Hue-manity (see Human Being, p. 71) is conditioned to seek happiness. The motivation is to be unhappy and therefore seek. As soon as we are happy, we default to unhappiness again to continue the search. As in "Too good to be true." It actually looks more like we seek misery.

Getting around this is easy. There is only the now. If we seek happiness in each individual "now," we will remain in perpetual bliss. Remember, the new blessing may not even resemble the old blessing. In every moment there is always a new blessing/bliss. What is the blessing in this now? This is for you!

Appear: It would appear that in using the word *appear*, one allows reality a fluidity. In this way, one aspect after another can be seen. Nothing is locked in place. Appear is used not for a lack of commitment or as denial, but rather for a greater seeing. Things appear as they actually are when everything appears as love.

Ascending: Used to be an verb; now it's a noun. I am an ascending. If you are reading these words, you are an ascending. Walk like an ascending, sound like an ascending.

Attention: "Thought creates, and where you place your attention grows." This quote comes from author Drunvalo Melchizedek. I've also heard it as, "where thought goes, energy flows." Sacred attention is the *conscious* placement of one's attention. Where you place your sacred attention grows. For example, if you place your attention on how "hard" a thing is, then (by your command) it becomes far more difficult. If you place it only on what brings you joy, joy happens.

The most valuable thing a person owns is where his or her attention is placed. Self-love equals self-discipline. There is a single discipline: where attention is placed. When you place attention where someone else is placing attention, the combined field is that much more powerful.

Authority/Author: This equals *knowing*. To gain enough information on a subject is to "know" about it, and trafficking in such knowledge is a step in the direction of personal sovereignty. It means "without doubt." And I mean that.

Belief: Your beliefs create your reality. You choose your beliefs. Therefore you choose your reality.

My belief in unity far exceeds my belief in separation. This allows me to see all things as a single universe and at the same time divided up into each of our individual universes.

A belief is a mirror. Whatever the belief is, it is reflected back to you in everything. You see what you believe. Thus, if someone believes in extraterrestrial crafts, such things will be seen by that individual.

Beliefs create reality. If something is not manifesting, there is a belief standing in the way. Change this belief now. Nothing is more than a belief away.

Birth trauma: Birth trauma and rebirthing are concepts brought to us by Leonard Orr. I recommend highly *Rebirthing in the New Age* and *Breaking the Death Habit*.

Rebirthing is a form of meditation that allows us to recognize an event in life (birth trauma) that programs our subconscious in a way that we do not prefer. It is the job of the subconscious to keep life normal, so if abuse occurs in life, it becomes "normal," and we are always creating abusive situations. The subconscious programming, thus recognized, can then be rewritten.

The birth trauma of modern man is the crucifixion of Christ. The rampant guilt manipulation that appears to be running our world is a reaction to the death of Christ. This mass subconscious programming has resulted in our putting to death almost everyone who has arrived here to lead us out of darkness. Copernicus, Galileo—the list is rather extensive.

The birth trauma of many countries on our planet is

war. Therefore war is normal on our world, and will continue so until we change this.

Blessing: You. You are a blessing, a quintessential note in the universal symphony.

Everything that happens is a blessing. By this we mean to say *everything* is a blessing. It may take time to recognize a particular event as a blessing, nonetheless it is. You may leap forward by just knowing that whatever happens will turn out to be a blessing. Even if the unhealed ego won't recognize it immediately. Everything is a blessing no matter what it looks like. Remind children that they are a blessing and welcome in our world.

Breath: Breath is joy. (Cigarettes are irrelevant.) Fear tends to stop breath. (This is why we never hear someone who falls off a tall building stop their scream to inhale and then continue to scream the rest of the way down.)

When you inhale and exhale, you are participating in natural laws of the universe. This is why many forms of meditation have to do with conscious breath. Children take a kind of conscious breath, a sigh, when they are full. This is a satisfaction breath. Right now inhale until your lungs tickle. Then let go with a pleasure sound. Voila, satisfaction. This may be repeated any number of times. It is both meditation and release. With the release comes more room for even greater satisfaction.

Cancel: In the growth of our relanguaging, we may say something that we would prefer not to say. In case you say a disempowering word, just say "cancel." This is the void code. It tells the universe to return the command to the void from whence all things come.

As you recognize the deep-seated subconscious programs functioning in your current life, use the word "cancel" to turn them off. You may then rewrite the counterproductive programming. Be kind to yourself at all times. We have been trained in the opposite direction. Cancel is the off switch, the verbal veto. Enjoy it.

Change: Change is the one constant. Fight it and be swept away. It is not a matter of *if* we will change, it is a matter of *when* we will change.

We fear change because of the uncertainty; we embrace change because of the freedom. There is no such thing as uncertainty; denial yes, uncertainty no. Those who change freely will lead those who change timidly.

"I change effortlessly by grace." This is a great first building block of new consciousness. It is giving yourself permission to change. Change will increase with grace and ease when one incorporates "I delight to adjust my flight." Change is evolution. It is our great friend. Embrace it. Celebrate diversity.

Charisma: By definition, the word means "Christlike." The more loving one is the more charismatic one is. Part of love is self-love, an important part. Self-love defines self-image. The more you love yourself, the more lovable you are.

Choice: Free will means choice. You always have choice and since choice by its nature is a plural, you always have more than one choice. Once you have made a choice, you can, at any time, make a different choice.

We choose what thought is going through our mind at every moment. We choose where our attention is placed at all times. When this principle is mastered, we experience the true power available to us.

Command: We are so powerful that we are capable of giving commands. These commands are rooted in decision. When we decide something and do not doubt it, it happens. Command the arm to move and it does. Doubting this command is called multiple sclerosis. The decision is the fuel. Decide, then allow the unfolding; this is command.

Commitment: To have commitment is to be on your own side, to be loyal to yourself. Even the airlines tell you to put the oxygen mask on yourself first, otherwise you are likely putting it on your orphan.

Commitment is magic. It is the life force. Once committed to yourself, the electromagnetic field around your body—the auric field—gives off permission for others to cooperate with you. To take emotional responsibility for others is to omit taking care of ourselves, to give our energy to every little energy theft that comes along. Write: "It is to myself that I am committed," a hundred times.

Confidence: This is trusting in ourselves. It is easy when we accept our own nature as divine. Without doubt, there is no other nature (see Trust, 89).

Death: Free will does not stop at the moment of death. It doesn't stop right before it either. Free will doesn't stop after death. Free will doesn't stop.

We choose the moment of our death. No matter what it looks like. God may have a list, but it is a list of when we decide to die. The exact number of people who have had their life cut short is zero.

It is comforting to think of each of us as having completed our life's evolution in exactly the right amount of time. A young person who has passed may have had only to receive love; this fulfilled all that they have to do.

To believe in others determining one's death is to believe in victimism. We create far more than is realized. Having decided to die, one's auric field—the electromagnetic field around the body—could attract a "stray" bullet. Likewise, with "no decision to die" the bullet would be deflected by the auric field. Therefore, if you have not decided to die, then have no thought of it.

Decision: Choice and decision are the functioning of free will. The one and only thing people ever do is decide. Once the decision is made, it is carried out by the automatic universe. Decide something, pause, and watch it glide into place. You may have heard people say, "The hardest part of the whole project is the decision." Observe: The easiest part of the project is the decision.

The decision is the activator code for the universe. We are the activator code for the universe. We make decisions. Initialization begins the moment that we decide something. Where we place our attention provides the focal point for the all that is. When we decide something and then place our attention on doubt, the doubt takes the place of the decision. The doubt becomes the new decision. It automatically voids the original decision.

"Absolute Decision" is a decision that is not doubted. Some decisions never manifest because of some internal conflict. An absolute decision is decided and known. It is a decision by someone who is sovereign of their faculty. All of us are capable of this; we just never had a name for it. Decision is power. Decision is a form of love.

Desire: Do-Sire. To do what you love the most. Decision precedes desire. We decide to have a desire. Pretending desire is "random" or that it just drops in full blown is just a game.

Destiny: As a word of power it is synonymous with choice. Destiny equals choice. We always choose our destiny, always. The only other definition of destiny is evolution. Evolution is the one and only true destiny of humanity. There is no such thing as predestination. We would all be automatons.

Destiny as a word of power refers to the freedom of choice inherent in the concept of free will. Destiny means opportunity. Any moment in time that we choose is our turn up to bat. We each individually create our destiny. Our destiny does not create us.

Dismiss: *Dis* is to have no respect. *Miss* is where it doesn't hit. To dismiss is to have no respect for something that does not hit. We receive very little information/education on the subject of dismissing anything. If someone insults us, we take it to the grave. We can simply and summarily dismiss anything we choose.

65

For something to leave our thinking by our command is to not be guilty about it. If it is an insult, a slight, then it is that person talking about themselves to themselves, right in front of us, pretending they are addressing us. Get over it. Do not be so easily hurt. The moment you take it personally, the creation of your life is turned over to someone else.

With no ability to dismiss, the altercation is turned into a tape loop and slowly fades, over the years. Is amnesia our only recourse? What nonsense! Dismiss it if it comes back, then examine the true hook. This "true hook" is guilt about your performance in the event. Have a little personal power; have a huge amount of personal power. You are not guilty! Make choices not defaults.

Do: There is an echelon of freedom inherent in the realization that things are done through us, not done by us. When they are done by us there is an endless stream of tasks. Once it is realized that things are done through us by the universe, then the only "effort" is the decision.

Dominion: It is said quite eloquently by Paul Hawken in his book *The Magic of Findhorn*, "To have dominion means to understand completely, to have sympathy, to love, to enter into a state of wholeness and perfect harmony with all creation."

There is an idea that dominion is Do-Minion. When I ask the word *dominion* to present itself to me, I see *in domino*. From this I can see nature as described by the domino effect, which is balance. As long as we achieve balance we are in dominion.

Door: There is a holy man who suggests that as long as we separate meditation from the rest of our life we are essentially not being meditation, we are doing meditation. In order to further integrate meditation into our lives, consider any physical door in your life. When we meditate by saying that every time we walk through any door we enter into a place of greater clarity, then our lives are perpetually upgrading. A car door is a excellent one. The whole concept is a-door-able.

Economics: The word *economics* means the echo of the name, echo of man. The study of economics is the study of where and how people place their attention. All of the study of economics is this simple. Where are people placing their attention? The power of so many of us placing our attention on a given belief has yet to be explored as the miraculous resource that it is.

Edge: The frontiers of consciousness always have new ground. The way to ensure exploration is to move forward by releasing or giving away all that we have previously gathered. This makes room for more clothes in our closet. *There is always more edge to cut.*

Some Native Americans do the turkey ceremony in which all that one has is given to other tribe members. This makes way for the new to enter our lives.

Life on edge? Sit and write, in long hand, one thousand times: "It is OK to move away from the edge."

Effortlessness: Effortlessness is achieved when we realize that all things are done through us, not by us.

Emotion: Our emotions are simply our energy motions. Our motivations are in line with our emotions. So when our emotions move us, we can begin to create instead of simply acting out unconscious behaviors.

Entertainment Committee: One of the many things we may ask the universe to do is to entertain us. Appoint a group of five guides to be your personal entertainment committee. Just say, "OK, Entertainment Committee, you're on." Place your attention elsewhere for a moment and then come back and . . . voila!

The first time I consciously activated the Entertainment Committee was in a restaurant. A few tables away were four men who looked like bodybuilders. They were all blonds and there were about nine hundred Heineken bottles on their table. I assumed they were German weightlifters in town for some exhibit. I'm sitting there eating my soup and I think, "OK, cue the Entertainment Committee," and suddenly they broke into song in Swedish. They were a barber shop quartet singing "Daisy." I ended up laughing so hard I couldn't get my breath.

Epic hero: I am my own. Say it: "I am my own epic hero." *Hero* can be pronounced "her-o" when referring to a female incarnate. Each of us writes every monologue that comes out of our mouth. Write yourself a leading part in life. A staring role. Don't allow people to cast you in a bit part in their script.

This word can result in your power being externalized. Considering what a hero would do in any situation can be valuable counsel. The point is what will *you* do in this situation. There is no one who is not a hero.

Epiphany: We study for years. We can repeat all the information. The epiphany is the moment we get it. Something suddenly goes up online. We begin to live the life of it, not just know of it. Install a software program and your computer has an epiphany. It's the same for your brain. Just call for one. It's like a catharsis on wheels. It's a conscious point in time that is used to mark the stair step and plateau that is evolution.

ETC: Extraterrestrials are real and so are their craft. When we call something "unknown" or "unidentified," we automatically file it in a place in our mind we may never find again. The expression "UFO" keeps us from remembering our sighting. We may do better calling these vehicles "ETC," Extraterrestrial Craft.

Evolve/Evolver: Eve Love/Ever Love. We are evolvers. It's what we're designed to do. Love is evolution. The first four letters of *evolution* spelled backward is *love*. One more letter and it is *u-love*. Still further and it is *[K]no[w]-it-u-love*.

Evolution is adaptation. Adaptation is change. We will evolve; this is a given. Everything we are, whatever happens, it is all our evolutionary movement forward.

The shark is a truly magnificent model. It must constantly move forward. It is the design of the animal; the gills must be provided with a stream of fresh water in order for the shark to live. We are like this. We are constantly moving forward, constantly striving to be better. The thought is efficiency. Our language is full of eddies. While it is always moving forward, overall, word/thoughts can delay us.

Faith: *Faith* is another word for *knowing*. Faith could be called future knowing in the present. As knowing is the opposite of doubt, faith is the opposite of fear. There is no such thing as a little faith.

Faith is knowing that everything is perfect. Anything that happens is the next step forward, despite what we have trained our senses to report. Faith is the celebration of new consciousness, new freedom. The more faith we have, the less brain space is taken up by chatter.

Fear: I am no longer afraid to be fearless. Some words are both power words and slave terms, depending on the connotation. I am going to speak (actually write) the word *fear* as a word of power. "Hello, my old friend fear." Fear, by its nature, separates. When we expand our circle of influence to include this word, it no longer has the ability to enslave. We become the master. Fear serves us by revealing deeper recesses of our own being. It is also useful in developing the muscle that dismisses nonsense.

Fixed purpose: We may choose a fixed purpose. I once planned a seminar on past lives. No one showed up, despite promises. The fear spiral that resulted set off the failsafe. When I thought the command "highest possible thought," I found myself in the office of Christ with a secretary telling me that my appointment is now.

Then, I am suddenly walking next to "The Man" Himself. He says we're going to the year 800. We come upon a barbarian. He is five feet tall by five feet wide by five feet thick. In fact, thick does describe him—an I.Q. in the seventies. He has a tree branch as a club and he is pounding on a huge wooden door of some cottage. People are inside bracing the door. Nothing short of a bazooka will stop him. Since this is the year 800, there is no such thing as a bazooka. Nothing is going to stop him. What does he have? It is similar to faith; it is fixed purpose.

When we doubt, nothing is fixed. The barbarian never considered any other outcome. Therefore, there wasn't any doubt. He just knew. Anytime we make a decision without even thinking that it might go another way, an absolute decision, it is called fixed purpose; no other outcome even crosses the mind. (Thanks J.C.)

Frequency (higher and lower): When two people of different frequencies meet—one of a higher frequency and one of a lower—one of three things will happen. One, the person of higher frequency will maintain his or her frequency and the person holding the lower frequency will entrain up to the higher rate. Two, the lower-frequency person will leave instead. Or three, the higher frequency will drop down to the lower. This is called an argument, or homicide.

In other words, if you go into the office and everyone is a low gossipy frequency, then you have the choice to entrain down to it; the other choice is holding the higher frequency. As (r)evolutionary as this sounds, if we make the choice to maintain the higher frequency, the entire world will have to entrain up.

Fulfillment: Jackie Onassis said it very well with, "You can never be too thin or too rich." By logic alone it becomes visible that neither the path of glamour nor the path of materialism will put us in a position to reach fulfillment.

The ability to fill our potential is fulfillment. Flow is to be considered in this process, like abundance, like breath, like the ocean; there is the flow in and the flow out, and somewhere in between there is balance, fulfillment, satisfaction.

Futuring: There are those who say that all music, all literature, already exists. Simply go there and bring back a piece of art, or for that matter, science. Decide something in the future. Lazarus, a conscious channel in San Francisco, suggests envisioning something in the future so that current reality is pulled to it. We've all done this; there just hasn't been this explanation for it. Personally I've decided to found and build a forty-story pyramid dedicated to the advance of human thought.

Genius: When we recognize the obvious, we have genius. The simplest solution is inherently the better solution. Water runs down hill in the most direct path. It does this every time, no exceptions. Water is a genius. We are made mostly of water, therefore we are inherently of genius. The army with the simplest uniform wins. The shortest distance between portal A and portal B is no distance. Simplicity rules. The list goes on and on.

Gift: Hunbatz Men in his book *Secrets of Mayan Science/Religion*, suggests that the Spiral, the spiral that is in all things, has been translated from glyph to glyph into the modern G. It represents the all. Our Mayan would further suggest the modern T represents man himself or herself.

In the word *gift*, *if* separates God (G) from Man (T). *If* equals doubt. Therefore, doing the math, knowing that *if* always means "make a decision," I come to the conclusion that I accept my divine gift, and thank you.

Gratitude: Gratitude is magic, the activator code for our universe. It converts any situation into joy. When we are grateful, things move toward us. When we are ungrateful, things move away.

When we see that things are done by us and that everything happens to facilitate our evolution, then we can be grateful for everything that happens, even if we don't recognize why. Everything upgrades. I am grateful that this book is read. I am grateful it isn't.

If we are grateful for anything that happens, knowing that whatever it is, it's our next step toward divinity, then we will never again be disparaged. Be thankful for everything, or be miserable; choose.

Guides: Spirit guides are beings who have completed their incarnational epoch. Guides are parts of ourselves that we have lost direct contact with. Contacting in this case equals calling. Call a guide for any purpose. Call a guide to assist with receiving, with joy, with clarity, the faculty of new methods of thinking. The universe is at our service.

Healing: There is nothing that is not healing. Healing is relanguaging. For example, they are not bugs, not germs; they are pets, companions. They are fun. Now we wish to have some other fun. Thank the "germs" for their service and dismiss them.

Healing is the act of self-sovereignty in which you tell your body it is time to get well *now*. The idea of illness is boring! Healing is fulfillment, happiness, evolution.

"Healing tones" are the vowel sounds spoken/sung in a ceremonial way. They will move energy blocks effortlessly. Sing the vowels at the top of your lungs with your arms moving slowly like wings. Close your eyes and feel the energy patterns, the paths in your body change.

Healing tones can also be just speaking in your healing voice, any sound that you love, the sounds from a singing quartz-crystal bowl, any music Mozart ever wrote.

Heart brain: The ancient Egyptians believed that the heart is the organ that does the thinking. We have all seen this. A group of scientists were asked to have their heart affect an allegedly "random" number generator. It did have an effect. Here is proof. Feelings are a force to be reckoned with. Our brain speculates and our heart knows.

Human being: Man + Hue. A being of color. First of all we are human *be*ings. We may not serve ourselves well when we become human *do*ings.

This word has been used as a term of abuse: "I'm only human." This is spoken by someone on the path of regret (see "The Path of Regret," p. 144). Imagine our beautiful *human* used as an excuse for poor performance! Only human? There is nothing mere about a human.

The term *human-being* has long been confused with the concept of human doing. We are not our experiences. We are our evolution. We are Hue-man, beings of color. And it isn't just our auras, either; we have different skin colors, also. *Human* is restored to a sacred term.

Humility: True humility is knowing who it is that you really are. If all of the fear-based training stands in the way of this knowing, then write "I remember who it is I really am" a thousand times.

Intelligence: The ability to recognize and seize opportunities that serve us. Carpe diem. Intelligence is inherent in all things. It is the by-product of evolution. It is to know; it is the art of applying attention. Intelligence as wisdom is knowledge applied. Intelligence is "internal tell"—internal telepathy—which is the importing of a greater knowing from the part of us known as the rest of the universe.

Joy: *Love* is the only word I know of that can express the essence of joy. We all have individual and unique moments of joy. The French say "joie de vivre," the joy of life. It is true, to be alive is to love. Appoint your inner child to CEO of your entire group of spirit guides. The joy within will notice traction.

To those naysayers who say "you 'can't' always be experiencing joy," I say: (1) The slave word *can't* tipped me off. (2) Exactly how much non-joy am I to experience before I can experience joy? (3) I submit that in this lifetime alone I have experienced plenty of non-joy, in fact enough for an inexhaustible supply of joyousness. I choose infinite joy (see Annanda, p. 58).

Karma: Many people view this as a slave word. The picture of endless drudgery moving a wheel of endless debt is not really attractive.

Somewhere in time *karma* became mispronounced. It's pronounced "harmony." What harmony you give off is the harmony that comes back. This is a harmony universe.

Give off the hatred/anger harmony and you experience a world filled with hatred/anger. Further, when we says something is going to be "hard," then it actually becomes "hard." Just as when we say something is easy it becomes easy. This is the principle of karma.

Knowing: To know something is to know it in every cell in your body, not just intellectually. In yoga we can know the various poses, but until we apply them, experience them, grow with them, there isn't much traction. Knowledge applied is wisdom. The famous brain/blood barrier isn't just for chemicals.

We can collect information and know why something happens. Can we also know something without knowing why we know it? To know something involves a decision. The decision process does not require a body of evidence to function. One may simply know something. Know your knowing. When we can know without knowing why, we begin the path of being instead of the path of doing. Knowing without "why" is called faith (see Faith, p. 70).

Laughter: The interdimensional reset that eases every situation. Call the gift of being a comedian. It's just that easy.

Remember, the funny stuff must be true. If it isn't true, it isn't funny. And if it isn't funny, it isn't healed.

Life: The art of the placement of attention. The art of decision. The gift of breath. A way of thought. Don't be so deluded as to believe that your life is in charge of you. Thank you for remembering that you are in charge of your life.

Light/Darkness: The Essenes were a people who worshiped God as darkness. Now, before the twenty-first-century mind goes haywire, please consider that light by its nature must have a source and is therefore not so infinite. Darkness is everywhere, always; much more Godlike, eh?

This darkness is like the no-thing mentioned by Osho. In meditating to experience this darkness, I arrived at a place in my thinking that is like a black hole in my mind. Were I insulted, the insult would be routed directly into this exit and leave me free of annoyance.

(By the way, the Essenes eventually had a second civilization grow up next to them. This group was referred to simply as the Herd. After a while, the Herd was absorbed into the older civilization and the combination civilization was called the Essenes, But Not Herd.)

Love: It is the key. You may run any scenario again and again. It is only when you choose the most loving response possible that things actually move forward. The movie *Groundhog Day* illustrates this quite well. Time moved forward only after the Bill Murray character loved himself enough to be kind and loving to everyone around him.

Everything is love. Anything that anyone does is an act of love. It is a matter of having the senses to perceive it. Whatever is done to a child, that child translates it as love. When the child grows up, the adult acts out whatever the input was, thinking that this is love. All of the abuse in our genetic line could be ended in a single generation. I will credit the Aboriginals with having the great technique of child rearing. "Never speak harshly to a child." Therefore the children grow up to be quite lovely.

Some of us love to "hate." A transparent effect, considering that whatever we hate is what we do not like about ourselves.

The only word that I have found to be synonymous with love is risk. In order to experience love the way the conscious mind thinks of it, take a "chance." Those of us who have been hurt in love so many times in so many past lives, reincarnate unwilling to take any risk. This is called low blood pressure. Their bodies won't come up with the juice to enter the game. When you talk to God after your death, be able to say, "I took a chance and I was in love sixty seconds before I lost 'em." It beats zero. To paraphrase John Lennon: Love is all there is.

Master: A master is one who walks the middle of the road. This road is in the land beyond right and wrong. A master is one who has left the valley of the shadow, who has outgrown guilt. A master who acted guilty would no longer be a master.

A synonym for *master* is *balanced one*.

Meditation: I remember a part of me that is my guide for meditation. This part of us is built in. One of the simplest forms of meditation is to simply count breaths. There are other ways that are just as much a built-in part of us. Another word for *meditation* is *listening*. Sit quietly, close the eyes, ask a question. The answer that comes may be a surprise.

In the beginning meditation is something we do. We set aside time that is just for ourselves. This time grows until finally we aren't *doing* meditation, we *are* meditation. We never leave this state.

Micro/Macro: The small affecting the large is a very big deal. The micro *is* the macro. This is called Lorenzo's Butterfly Effect—a butterfly flapping its wings creates a hurricane somewhere else. There is a much bigger scenario. An ancient teacher suggests that when the human race was given permission to discover and use nuclear power for the purpose of ending WWII, it was like giving a hand grenade to a three year old. Something was done to balance this. This something is quite visible. It is the color purple. There has been more and more purple appearing in our world. Even the rainbow is different than it was fifty years ago. This increase in purple is a design to advance our spirituality. At one time only a king was allowed to wear purple. Now, even the most conservative among us wear purple. This purple effect was a decision made by our galaxy, well, actually the government of our galaxy.

Nature: To see nature as a force raging against us is to fail to recognize ourselves as this force. An entire community "forced" itself to take a few days off—the force of a snowstorm, that is. Nature is on our side; Nature loves us. As we begin to get to know our universe, we recognize just how much it loves us. Nature is a perfectly maintenance-free environment. Mankind strives for such a thing to no avail.

"Human Nature" is the nature of the Family of Humanity. Our nature is magical. Our nature is God nature. We create with our very thoughts. It is our nature to be true to ourselves.

No: No is an extremely powerful word. It is not difficult to say "No." It is also not difficult to say "No" without any guilt. When you experience a situation where love is directly expressed by saying "No," then own it. Saying "Maybe" is not a substitute.

It is worthy of note that if one doesn't say "No," the other person will continue to suck energy, tangle, blither, and so on, until borders are created. Borders are created and installed the moment this two-letter word is uttered. When "No" is pronounced with authority, the person does not continue to ask. Authority does not mean anger or force; it means knowing.

When someone says, "May I ask . . . ?" "No" is a perfect answer. "May I ask" is one of the many linguistic devices that puts us to sleep.

Non-Speech: Being truly conversant with one's diplomatic skills involves the art of knowing when not to speak. Non-speech isn't not knowing what to say, it is not uttering some unconscious guilt acquiescence. Many times things will go the way we wish when we simply keep our mouth shut. Not speaking is very powerful.

Obedience: The following is paraphrased from *The Urantia Book*.

Usually when we reach about 2,190 days of age, around age six, we make our first moral decision in life. It is at this point that we have a being called a "Thought Adjuster" assigned to us. This is a being different from our companion angel. This being is connected on one end to God and on the other end to us. We each have our own personal one. This being, also called our "Mystery Monitor," has a single job description: to bring us back home to God.

Now let's say that we are all in the same boat. We can call this boat the mind. The captain of our boat is our free will. The pilot of the boat is the Thought Adjuster. Quite naturally the pilot will do whatever the captain says. It is at exactly this point that God gives up his will to us.

This idea got me over the fear of the expression "doing God's will." Who wouldn't actively seek the advice of the pilot? He has the map. Quite assuredly God does love you. God loves us all. This means that everything that happens is in our best interest. Think of how free this makes us!

Om: You are Om-ing. As you Om, you begin to travel back in time, traveling through all the monks that ever Om-ed. Finally you get to the very first monk. It turns out that he was surprised when he was asked to lead the first meditation. So he stood up and in collecting his thoughts said, "Ummm . . ." only, in his language, it was pronounced, "Omm . . . " It just caught on. When we Om, it opens and balances our chakras (energy centers), thus opening us to a higher consciousness.

Opinion: Opinion is the nature of the functioning of any particular brain. It is the very essence of thought. It precedes desire. It is certainly not to be referred to as "only." One of the most ridiculous disclaimers is "only an opinion." When the word *opinion* is used without *only*, the effect is remarkably powerful. This is because *opinion* refers to brain process in a nonjudgmental way. People have an inherent respect for another's opinion when it is phrased this way. Another opinion is always welcome.

Opinion as "insult": Whenever people intend to insult us, the opinion they express is really their opinion of themselves. Seeing such comments in this light actually gives us a *great deal* of insight about their lives. Which will probably be much more than we are interested in.

There are soon to be 7 billion of us on this planet. This means there are 7 billion opinions. Out of all these there is one and only one valid opinion of you. This is your opinion of yourself. All the other opinions are really other individuals' opinions of themselves; they actually have nothing to do with you.

Parenting: Parenting would be completely different were we raising adults instead of raising children. Because our society at this time runs on a codependent matrix, chil-

dren remain dependent on parents. A more fulfilling parenting means creating a loving environment and then
landing a being(s) in it. We support them totally at first
and then gradually educate the children in such a way that
they become self-existing, that is, adult.

We are all capable of being our own loving parent. We
may get in touch with an internal nurturer as well as an
internal loving father. We can also have a good childhood
any time we choose by simply rewriting it—by choosing to
view it differently: "I created such a rough childhood, so I
could become self-reliant."

Passion: Ah, passion. It is what drives us once we stop
being driven by guilt. What a delightful concept. Imagine
being activated by the love of doing something instead of by
the fear of not doing it. Passion equals balance. On the one
side is indifference, on the other is obsession, in the middle
is passion. Welcome to passion!

Power: Our power is our ability to generate love. Our
power is identical to the power of God. We are all love-
generating beings. See the cute bunny? The world is
instantly a better place because we imagined the bunny.
Whenever we create love, we are quite powerful. Whenever
we generate fear, we are not so powerful. Love is our very
nature, our power.

Power is concisely described as where we place our
sacred attention. Another way of saying this is creativity.
Our power is our creativity. We are all imaginatively and
beyond imaginatively powerful.

Pretend: Pretending is the imagination's sibling. To pretend is to lend action to the imagination. It is the doing, the electron in the magnetic field.

You can use pretending as a tool: Pretend you can do it. Or pretend that you can pretend you can do it. Pretend is the imagination in an active form.

Re-: Words that start with "re-" suggest that placing the sacred attention more than once is necessary. Cognizing these words can accelerate self-awareness, thus making only one attention necessary to get the growth accomplished.

"Rebate": To be baited by advertising is not enough. We must now be baited again by the lure of getting our own money back. Rubbish!

"Recognize": To know again. It's done with your cognitator.

"Refuse": To replace a fuse. Were we to decide to not do something to begin with, in order to not be drawn into the situation we would leave the original fuse intact. One might say, "I fuse to do it."

"Repair": To reunite with one's resources (pair again).

"Represent": To present again.

"Resent": All the information, the experience itself, must be re-sent. Didn't get it the first time. We may add that the original information will be re-sent again and again until the human catches on. Therefore, the more re-sent-full you are, the more times the experience will be replayed, each time at a louder volume. When we resent we enter into a mind-set where some tape loop takes up hours, days, weeks and may replay years from now (see Tape Loops, p. 145).

"Resist": To re-insist. When we place our attention on anything, we increase it. Therefore, "resistance is futile." If one continues to resist, then resistance is funereal. Tell whatever it is to go away, then choose something very happy to place attention on, pause for the gap, and then watch whatever it is dissipate. The word *resist* is a trick that places the sacred attention on what we wish to dismiss.

"Resolution": To solve again.

"Resource": To go to the source again. Each of us individually is the source. All of us have all the resources necessary to be magnificent if we choose. Were this not true, we would have a "re-sorcerer," instead of a sorcerer. I am the source! Say it out loud.

"Respect": To look again.

"Retire": To tire again, because we aren't tired enough after a life of work. Don't retire. Decide to have a brilliant future after leaving the work force. (That's actually forced work.)

"Retreat": To treat yourself in a different way—to treat again. When you're done beating yourself up, you remember to go somewhere and treat yourself well again.

"Return": To take the next turn. On and on.

Please feel free to translate any other "Re" code in our language by your own authority.

Sacred: Set apart; somehow hidden by a cloak. Sacred information is not purposefully kept from us, as with secrets. This time it is education, or the lack of it, that creates the veil.

We do not place a two-year-old in front of a brand-new computer. Certain cognitive skills are required to operate the device. Likewise, sacred knowledge requires time and education. The true nature of the sacred is in the knowing. Sacred isn't scare-y.

The sacred requires a specific mind-set to recognize its true potential. It is revered for its "hidden" power. When a mystical knowledge is brought into focus, an interdimensional door opens. This door is opened and the power of the sacred activated by the knowledge of how to do it and by placing our attention on it. Therefore, human attention is also sacred.

Select: Self-elect. To select refers to electrons. When we place our attention on something, electrons begin to flow in it. To select it is to turn it on. Nothing exists without someone placing their attention on it. Use instead of *need/want*.

"E-lect": Same process, only there is a computer involved (Ha-ha).

Silence: The place in the mind that each of us has that is our personal temple. Go into this place. There is not even you speaking. Even with noise going on in the room. Still, simply silence. This is more easily achieved when we know that we are not required to always participate with the outside. When one believes this, one will see it—I mean not hear it. One doesn't have to go deaf to achieve silence.

Numerous orders of monks have found value in the tradition of the vow of silence, as have couples who have lived together without a word for long periods of time. As far as the couple is concerned, the vow of silence is better serving as an action, than re-action.

When we stop the output, it turns up the input. In this way it's like losing a sense. The silence allows us to hear about our causative relationship with the environment.

Speak: To perform the sacred act of manifesting a thought. It is the essence of our command protocols. If we speak a negativity it solidifies it in our lives and bodies. If we speak an acknowledgment of what appears to be a negativity and next banish it, then it is banished.

Both speech and thought are capable of manifestation. We think at a different frequency than we speak. Let us say that we think in the fourth dimension, and when we speak, it steps thoughts down and locks them into the third dimension. Efficiency would look like preparing a thought in the fourth dimension and then speaking it, thus commanding its existence. Speech can then be viewed as a sacred act, and therefore sovereign. (Speech is already sacred.)

Speaking all the time is a form of speech disorder that may not yet be fully recognized. People who must speak constantly do so because they are very uncomfortable with themselves. When we are silent, we hear our inner voice.

This inner voice is something which serves us very well (see Silence, p. 86).

Stimulating: *The Urantia Book* refers to us as divine beings. It provides us with a viable word to refer to discordant situations without giving up our power by calling things difficult, hard, exasperating, and so on. As we have suggested, labeling a situation as "hard," gives it command to become even more difficult. When referring to such a circumstance, just say it is "stimulating." For example, "The study of higher mathematics is quite stimulating." When one encounters a situation that is "difficult" and refers to it as "stimulating," it becomes an entirely different experience.

When one encounters a situation that is "difficult" and refers to it as "stimulating," it becomes an entirely different experience.

Synchronous: The entire universe is perfectly synchronized with itself. Put any two liquids in a glass and they will synchronize, come to balance. Since our reality is constantly being created by us, "reality" is always synchronizing with us, entraining to us. *Synchronous* is a word of power; *coincidence* isn't.

Telepathy: I knew you'd look this one up. Telepathy is the human ability to link minds. All human beings are telepathic. In fact we are highly telepathic. The level of doubt and low self-esteem rampant in our world used to keep this from being as usable as it could be, even visible. When we love each other, there is an automatic link up. When we finish each other's sentences, it's not one brain being faster than the other; it's just sending and receiving. It's more than feeling the other, it's knowing the other's whereabouts, mood, even what the other is looking at through his or her eyes. This is true for all of us all the time, and it is true even if we don't know the other person. We are limitless creators. We are all perfectly telepathically connected. Doubt only appears to take it back.

Thank you: The traditional religious idea of God wanting to be praised is to me confusing, as I feel that God in the absolute does not exist in any state of want. However, I do recognize that the universe works on a profound principle of gratitude. In other words, a state of gratitude equals a state of bliss, Annanda. Live in a constant state of gratitude and watch the magic enter your life. What is there not to be grateful for?

In French, "thank you" is *merci*. The universe exists always in a state of mercy, thank you.

Trespassing: is forgiven. This is to be a policy that one lives by. Understand that sacred space is by invitation only. When you believe this, it is true. Not believing that our beliefs create our reality is how we are kept in slavery. In living this paradigm, people who are invited come into your sacred space, no one else. On my front door appear the words: "Trespassing Is Forgiven, Enter at Your Own Risk."

Trust: To trust is to know. Trust is taken away from us at an early age. Perhaps the first time we are told that we have done something "wrong" or told "no." Our ability to trust becomes misplaced. Understanding that everyone can be trusted to be true to their own nature restores our ability to trust.

The concept then becomes our trusting of our own nature. When we master this knowing of our own nature, intuition about others becomes possible. Hint: We all have the loving nature that is God. No matter what happens, we act out what we think love is.

Having our trust taken away turns out to be the first step in our journey toward wisdom. When our trust is restored, when our innocence is restored, then we are both innocent and wise at the same time. To have trust about the future is to create the future by decision. The decision is predicated on knowing, and knowing is predicated on trust. In other words, if one knows that something will happen in the future, it will.

Truth: We all have our own truth. Our individual truth is always the correct one for us because our beliefs create our reality. Anything is true as long as it is believed to be true. We choose our beliefs, and as we choose different beliefs, truth modifies. The truth of a sixth grader is nothing like the truth of an undergrad. Since we all choose different beliefs, we all have different truths. There is nothing confusing about it.

The truth is always simple. The universe is all one thing, the periodic table not withstanding.

Unwind: This is a word of power once we realize that the *w* has been inverted. *Unwind* is really *unmind*. In order to unmind, you quiet your mind. Here we have a great deal of literary reference. The process has been called everything from relaxation to meditation to nirvana. To do it as a part of everyday life is to always be at ease with yourself.

Unwritten Law: Unwritten Law is a way of stating, recognizing, the subconscious programming visible in conscious life. It is the way in which our subconscious is wired into the creation of reality.

Personally I've decided to become an Unwritten Lawyer. The credentials are always spoken of highly.

Validation: Validation is assurance. Before we move forward we would prefer to feel sure of our steps. This sort of assurance comes from within. Validation can appear to come both from inside and outside. Which is more valid: internal validation or external validation? Trick question; there is no external. As we become self-loving, whole beings, validation becomes a given, and we have an infinite supply of self-validation on hand instantly.

Waveform generator: A mechanical device that emits a specific waveform(s). Nothing generates a waveform like a human being. We do it everyday, and we do it well; it's just that we don't know it. The holographic universe responds to every vibration (speech or thought) that we make— including doubt. Were we living on a planet where parents recognized and saluted their children's divinity, a child could decide that it will rain that day, give the command for it to do so, and then play elsewhere while the atmosphere prepared the downfall. This child wouldn't question whether it was going to rain. He'd just know it.

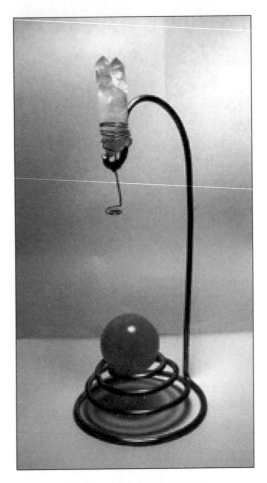

WAVEFORM GENERATOR

This is a waveform universe; all thoughts and intentions have a waveform. If you generate an intention, all like results will be drawn to you. If you magnify this intention with the crystal and send it out through the sphere, you are amplifying the intention. We know that wherever we place our attention grows. The waveform generator acts like a pattern buffer: it holds your intention in a particular place, leaving your mind free to place its sacred attention elsewhere. The original thought stored in the waveform generator continues to amplify the original intention. You are really amplifying this beyond measure because you have unified your power and externalized it in the waveform generator. While meditating, focus an objective into the device. As the harmonic returns, observe what happens. See www.telepathictv.com for more information on these.

Since we on this planet often doubt before we have even finished giving a command, a waveform generator can be used to obviate doubt. Place a clear command into a waveform generator and it will forever assist you in the manifestation of the command. They are thought amplifiers.

Whole: Independent, complete, self-existing, healing nicely, remembering fearlessness, better and better, ignited. In short, evolving.

On the flip side, when we feel incomplete, we have again been tricked into placing our most valuable attention on what we do not appear to have. Place your attention on the idea that we all individually and cumulatively have 100 percent of all that we require. We are whole. There is no one among us that does not have all that they require to succeed nicely.

Wish: Permission to give yourself something that you love. It is granted by the part of you that looks like the rest of the universe. Your wish is your command. We are borne with the power to wish things into and out of existence. Adults at first assist with this. Then they take it away. Their parents did it to them. It's some sort of a barbaric custom.

Yes: Yes is the key. Yes is a smile. Yes is the activation code. When we get to yes, any door opens. Say "yes" to you. Since the outside must reflect the inside, you already have the key to every opportunity. Yes you do.

The Dialect of Angelese
(Thank You Angels)

We all speak a language that is not commonly acknowledged. The language of the angels. Many of us have spoken of hearing the angelic choir. These ultradimensional vibrations have the ability to modify anything. We also have this ability. It is a language of sound and breath.

Remember when someone proposed something, and you just exhaled with a certain tone and everyone instantly knew that it would or wouldn't happen? This is Angelese. Begin to collect this language in your conscious mind. Start with just a pleasure sound on the breath. You could stop a rhino at full charge with it. This dialect is part of our soul's birthright. Reclaim it.

QUADRANT

3

LANGUAGE ANOMALIES

LANGUAGE ANOMALIES (there are a few . . .) are little glitches in the language. Well no, actually huge glaring glitches. Our thinking, when it is done in words, resembles mathematical equations. When we think in these word formulas and include one or more doubt words in the equation, the results may be highly irrational or flat-out gibberish. As we master the elimination of these misdirecting words, our thinking sharpens. It's automatic.

Our language is having quite a growth spurt. It's more than just the regional dialects, more than the younger generations translating into the next unique vernacular. It's everything, from science to new technologies to popular culture. We are adding new word-concepts, yet we are not discarding unusable words. It's time to consciously delete certain words and get out of the thought habits that these ridiculous words keep in place.

A few years ago a number of people began to stop using the word *try*. A lot of people have spontaneously stopped "shoulding" all over themselves. I mean "should" never comes out of their mouth. A few more monkeys and we've got it.

The Mechanics of Language

Were someone to say that his New Year's resolutions included smoking, gaining weight, and spending money in a useless fashion, everyone would agree that he would be able to keep them. The mechanics that create these behaviors are in place and functioning, and therefore likely to happen.

Yet we can recognize and change these behaviors. It is truly spoken that this machinery of our life is the result of our individual experiences. Nevertheless, when we truly recognize that the machinery is actually the language (words) that we think in, we no longer have to carry around our luggage of guilt.

The dynamic of language can move things closer to us or, equally effortlessly, move things away. Let's say we describe an object, while remaining at a constant distance from it, as "here" or as "there"; there's a universe of difference between the two ideas. This is a symptom of duality thinking, brought to us by our upbringing of speaking a polar language.

"This/that" is an example of the many little polar twins that exist in our language. "This" is closer, "that" is farther away, yet it is all here.

We vs. they; us vs. them. There is no they! There is only us. All people on this planet are directly our blood kin. There are no exceptions here. This is a very important language code, for as soon as there is a "they," we are fractured. There could be no war ever created without the concept of "them."

When we say "the other team," we are all participating in a sporting event. The minute the term "them" is used, a completely different frequency is created. Estrangement occurs. (And this is without the suggestion that the parents of the opponents were never married.)

We do the same thing when we dehumanize our fellow creatures with titles that move them out of our realm. Waiter, clerk, student, client, laborer, soldier, criminal, prisoner, patient, and so on. All these words put us out of touch. These dehumanizing terms subtract from the quality of life for everyone immeasurably. "Fred brought me lunch" vs. "the waiter served me lunch." Here is the place where the richness of life dissipates. No matter what the lunch consisted of, it is more interesting when Fred brought it. These are our mechanics. Consciously choose what they do.

The personal pronoun *I* is the most commonly used word in language. The use of this word separates; it places a single person separate from all others and in fact every-thing. "I" is the ego. It is the code that fractures us into individuals. In our evolution, as we become conscious of the idea that the universe is inside of us rather than the other way around, we begin using the word *we* in its place.

The Pitfalls of Superlatives

Superlatives limit us and raise stress levels. The phrase, "I'm doing my best" has never been the swiftest retort coined by humanity. "I'm doing better" is a much stronger statement to make.

Once you've gone to superlative, well, there's just no going back. It's like "game over." The superlative tricks us into playing the comparison game. Actually, everything else does not lose its value; it is just linguistically constructed as less. Superlatives are the cul-de-sac of the language, the very nature of inflation.

Taking the superlative out, the comparatives of the adjective *good* would be *better* and *better and better*. Better is actually better than best because you can always do better. When you always do best, what is there to strive for? Better is best, no doubt about it.

Are you familiar with the term *negative ego*? This is actually the part of us that "hates" us. All superlatives are constructed to serve the negative ego. Stop using superlatives. Calmness will ensue.

In my entire personal languaging, there is only one superlative entry. This is when I catch myself having a fear. I snip the stream of consciousness at the fear point and plug it back into My Highest Possible Thought. This technique has landed me in some outstanding spots (see Fear, p. 19).

The Disconnects

All doubts are disconnects. They disconnect us from our power. These are words and phrases in our language that serve to numb, to stop the flow of energy that is us, our universe. These concepts appear to be pulling us out of the now.

It is a very subtle disconnect; we are always taught to desire—to be somewhere else than where we are. We get good at it. Sometimes this serves us, sometimes not so much. Below are a couple of the disconnects in our language.

I think: Observing our language from a distance can be quite entertaining. We set up such elements of social doubt that an individual so bold as to say "I know something" lays himself open to attack. They could be *made wrong*! Oh, the ghastly horror of it. As though all of life were in accordance with the rules of Scrabble.

This fear of being made wrong causes a plethora of default codes in our language. So the strategy for this "Scrabble game of life" looks like: "I'll beat them to the punch by self-challenging and self-defaulting." This strategy of default is all within the single phrase "I think." This type of "I think" is used when we really know. As a result of doing this so easily, we live in a constant state of doubt.

Our language is a slave language! I'm sorry; that's so harsh. Our language is a slave language, *I think*. There that's better. Certain words do really little more than leave us powerless, *I think*. Do you see how the phrase *I think* has nipped the cajones right off that sentence? Every time we end a sentence with *I think*, the same thing happens to us. We are robbed of our knowing. We are robbed of our power by the habit of our language. Count the number of times in a day or a week that the phrase *I think* is used. Then divide personal power by that number.

I think is a default. Know something or don't know

something—and say something or don't say it. It is OK to know; it is OK not to know. *I guess* is even more eviscerating than *I think*. It is a resignation to self-doubt. Reply yes or no. Decide rather than doubt.

Living without our knowing can be haphazard. Knowing equals authority. Living never being allowed to know for sure is not living. Living with no personal authority is not living. Let us decide to know. It's easy. When we have no personal authority, our life becomes endless scrapes with external authority figures. Once you know your knowing, these scrapes stop.

Later, Could be, Maybe: We have been asked to do something/make a decision. These words are what we say to disenfranchise a child who has stated that he or she wishes to play in divinity. It is a way of not making a decision while retaining authority to make the decision. "Maybe," at first glance, is meaningless. It really means "No." It states that the speaker doesn't have the belief in self to simply say "No." These words disconnect the time line and urge the other person to attempt to convince. Replace with: "Not at this time." (This is a decision.)

Dialects of the Obsolete Paradigm

Our beliefs create our reality; we choose our beliefs. This was introduced by Seth during the 1960s in the series of books by Jane Roberts. Let's face it, our words actually talk us into creating certain beliefs, certain realities. As long as we use this obsolete language, we create reality with less than a full potential. The following are systems of word pat-terning that do not serve us. Dropping them makes move-ment forward effortless and powerful.

WORDS OF ATTACHMENT TO A SINGLE OUTCOME

Again this is a side effect of living a life that is a battle between right and wrong. The drill is simple. Look at the situation and say, "Bless it if it does work out and bless it if it does not work out." Actually sit and think of positive rea-sons why it is a blessing in the event that it doesn't work. We already know why it is a blessing if it does. Then say, "Bless it if it does; bless it if it doesn't"; then choose. Osho, in the *Book of Secrets*, suggests, "I am not certain, I am not uncertain, I am clear."

Denial: Denial is a form of knowing, just not a very serving one. As we know, denial happens when we don't like what is going on in our perceived reality. We refuse to accept and therefore put ourselves in a vulnerable position. Denial is, as such, attachment to some other outcome. Denial is therefore a word of compromise. It is a fuzzy knowing. *Appears, sup-pose*, the ever popular *guess*, and of course *I think* are all words of denial, and of course, they are the denial of our true power. Remember denial is knowing divided by doubt.

Disappointment: When one is pleased only by one out-come, most of life may appear to be disappointment. Disappointment is a total crash of happiness. It directs the sacred attention to something that was not appointed. It has no respect for what is appointed.

Thinking with a word like *disappointment* is rending. I define this word: "I didn't know I could be happy even though things turned out differently than I had first thought." What a pleasure it is not to think with a word like this. Recovery is instant in that there was no downtime generated to begin with.

Glitch/Hitch: These are negative ego words that indicate attachment to outcome. The principle is simple: If there is only one outcome that is pleasing, we unintentionally place our attention on resisting all other outcomes. With our precious attention placed thusly, who knows which outcome will receive the greatest funding. Glitch and hitch render us "helpless."

NONEXISTENT WORDS

Do not misunderstand; these words are information packets. Nonexistent words do create our reality. Once we arrive at knowing that our beliefs create our reality *and* we choose our beliefs, we can see that some of our words are, in a real way, not real. They are words that describe concepts that do not actually exist, that is, unless we believe they exist. Believing these concepts exist creates little cul-de-sacs in our thoughts, little blind dead ends in our minds.

Once we decide something is an "accident," we stop searching for the true cause and effect. *Accident* is a dead end because it won't lead us back to the realization that we are creating all of our reality. These words are weak little excuses. All of these words have in common that the power is languaged as outside of us.

In order to stop using these fictional words it will be necessary to stop thinking and believing in these obsolete paradigms. This is a list of "fake" words. Look at how easily we give our power to these lies and how easily we can give up the use of these words.

Accident: Let's say that years ago there was an "accident." Not just any accident but indeed a tragic accident. Now, with the perspective of years of healing about the accident, one can see tangible benefit(s) from the event. Certain blocks have been removed. In fact, without the "accident," there wouldn't have been all these wonderful beginnings.

There are no accidents. Everything is on purpose and turns out to be a blessing. It is just the element of time that is a factor in it not being an instant blessing. Well, one could just know that it is a blessing ahead of time (see Faith, p. 70).

Alone: Yeah, give it an attempt. Go on; be alone. There is no such thing as alone. Who is the person you tell that you are alone? This is actually your higher self. Those who walk around talking to "themselves" are actually talking to their higher selves. When we feel alone and this feeling is uncomfortable, it indicates that our own company is not acceptable. This fear of loneliness is just a self-love issue.

Chance: There is no such thing as chance because every thing happens perfectly. We know that we are creating 100 percent of our life. Anything that happens has an activator code somewhere. Therefore anything that would have been described as happening by chance is actually an unrecognized decision. Or more accurately, a decision not recognized as having been made.

To say something happened by chance is to suggest that no one and nothing is running the universe. It is a part of a language of excuse. Do not live in the agonizing paradigm that things happen haphazardly.

The expression "to take a chance" means to make a decision and do something. Ironically, the word *chance* is equated with the word *random* and therefore appears not to be governed by decision. One is tricked into effort without decision just as in the word *try*. It appears that we take power with one hand and throw it away with the other.

Coincidence: It's no coincidence that this word is in this list. The word is a word of doubt and denial. To say "coincidence" is to deny the existence of a bigger picture. In fact it could be said to be the "coin in dense," or perhaps co-in-denial (co-creating in denial). Notice that once the word *coincidence* is used the search discontinues.

An ideal replacement word is synchronicity. "How synchronous an event; I am seeing a larger pattern emerging." This is a thousand times more powerful than "What a coincidence."

Guilt: This word involves the belief that you and what you have done are less than divine. It is not true. When you recognize your divinity in whatever it is that you feel guilty about, you will be free. (The exact amount of time between the act that caused the "guilt" and recognition of its divinity is in exact mathematical proportion to how guilty you feel.)

Helpless: "I don't do helpless": spoken by Batman in the animated series *Batman Beyond*. The principle of free will states that we *always* have free will. Therefore we always have choice. Choice always means we have more than one thing to choose from. Batman made a choice and stated a creed. Helplessness exists only if you choose to believe it. Personally I'm going with Batman's modeling.

Mistake: "Take something that is amiss." There are no mistakes, and we no longer have to take it. It may look like a mistake, but it is just a matter of time until its perfection is realized. This is a word for those of us who have not left the unsafe world, who still believe things occur fraudulently. A good replacement is: "I took a more circuitous rout."

Random: When someone speaks this word, they are actually saying that they do not see the bigger picture. It is the belief that things can occur that are not divine, not part of a larger system. The idea that numbers can exist and not be in a sequence does not mean the numbers are at random; it means we have not yet seen the scope these numbers have.

Chaos is a part of the system, and therefore chaos is actually a part of order. Randomness implies that things can occur out of order or with no order. It's not possible; it doesn't even seem possible. We can easily recognize a greater order. Nothing occurs at random. Before it occurs in the third dimension, it first occurs in spirit (other dimensions). Spirit is very easy to understand. *Random* is another word designed to strip us of power.

Rat: Our noble animal companion, one of the only wild animals to inhabit our cities with us. Mother Earth requires the feet of four-footed creatures tracing certain delicate energy lines. To my knowledge this has not been recognized yet. Nonetheless, this is very real.

Rats are by far the most abused animal on this planet. I don't mean just the atrocities committed on lab rats. All rats everywhere. We are only as free as the most enslaved among us. We are only as evolved as we are compassionate.

Rat has been eating our garbage for so long he has lost knowledge of his true food. Just like us. Rat has taken on man's low self-esteem.

There is a happy community of squirrels living in our backyard. We readily feed them with an abundance of peanuts and whole slices of bread. Occasionally a squirrel will pick up a whole slice of bread and bound through the grass. It is a sight that is a delight.

One day a rat comes to live in the backyard. In fact, he brings his whole clan. At first the rat's happy for the few crumbs left by the diurnal squirrel population. Squirrel and rat meet around dawn, when they have the world to themselves. They become friends. They share the rich bounty. Rat stays up later and later. One day we see the two dining together in the open where all the human neighbors can see. The rat picks up a whole slice of bread and bounds through the grass. We burst into tears, because squirrel has taught his cousin self-esteem. Rat has forgotten shame. The rat was not fleeing, just dancing.

Unsafe: This is a very deeply programmed lie. One is always safe. It is not possible to not be safe. Of course one could pretend to be not safe. Why, escapes me. Of course one would still be safe. Someone who is involved in a "dangerous" profession comes home and he is then safe? Safe, back from the war and yet killed in a car collision. Safety is not where you are, it is that you are.

The word *safe* is used to manipulate and control, and it's very popular. We're being sold the feeling of not being safe. Stop watching the news. There is absolutely no danger of being swept up by the currents, because we are the currents.

Here's a fun game: Count the number of times in a week that you turn a key in a lock. Now take your power and divide it by that number. Consider the number of robberies all the key turning prevented. This number is zero. Even if it did prevent a robbery, everything is still safe.

Were I dead, I'd still be safe. Everything is the way it is, and we go on evolving. Couldn't be safer. Moving forward by watching one's ass is laughable. Laughable for anyone watching, that is. There is no such thing as unsafe.

Wait: How is this possible? Do you shut down the brain and enter stasis? If the word were used in a real language it would mean "opportunity to have time for oneself." Does a stoplight, a long line in a market, negate our creativity?

We may be asked to pause in our journey. This is in no way harmful. The line at the supermarket may be a device of torture or an opportunity for meditation. The choice is every individual's to make. If no choice is made, it may default through the negative ego and rage will be what goes through the mind instead of . . . well, what would we do with a mind? The potential of a mind will not *wait* because there is no such thing.

Waste: This is a very abusive, guilt-ridden little device of a word. Were we to "throw away" food, we would in actuality be returning it to the earth, probably feeding some animal/bacteria in the process. Our universe is recycling as such. There is benefit to everything. It is an impossibility to waste. No matter what, everything is in its perfect place.

Warning: Formatting thought, with the use of such a word may result in guilty, abused little thoughts running one's beauty and grace straight into the ground.

The Dialect of Belief Conflicts

We all manifest perfectly everything that happens in our lives at every moment. When we tell something to manifest that doesn't exist, we manifest a belief conflict. Someone might say, "I manifest candy." Yet the person's belief is that he doesn't deserve candy. So the question is not "Why didn't I manifest the confection?" instead it's "Why don't I deserve such a treat?" The information packets in some words automatically carry out this misfiring of our divine ability to manifest.

Depression: Depression indicates growth spiritually. The newly expanded person becomes a little cramped in their former life, built by the lower-frequency self. We give the command to shatter our former life in order to build the higher-dimensional life. The only thing is, we don't remember giving the command. We gave it; we just weren't aware of the power there is in thought. When conscious of the command, there is no conflict because the new life would simply manifest, just as planned.

Because we don't remember the command, we fall backward into a spiral of lamenting what would have gone on if things hadn't shattered. Because of this lamenting, we don't give the command to construct the new life. This is better known as guilt. No pills are required to put an end to this! Just stop being "the depressed you," and enthusiastically build the new life.

Being depressed also may indicate a misplaced commitment to create the future as though it were some exact part of the past. It's a repeated failure to begin the new building process. This is self-indulgence.

When you are depressed, you are remaining in the past at all costs, especially the cost of the people closest to you. The second time your friends hear about it, it becomes boring. By the third, fourth, and fifth times, they feel trapped and stop listening entirely. Calls are not returned. People pretend not to be home. No one visits. "Depressing": People who will not cease to tell you about everything that has shattered in their life.

Fight: When two individuals have a belief conflict (and poor social skills), the result ends in fisticuffs. Were our planet just a little more evolved, those around the two individuals in conflict would circumvent the altercation. Physical violence usually results in more violence and even more hatred. We are all one thing. One would not expect the kidney cells fight with the liver cells.

Illness: When the belief conflict is internal, it will manifest as sickness. The common cold is an excellent example. The belief conflict is that you are entitled to pursue joy, yet your boss tells you that you must come in to work. This manifests as a cold. Since it may not serve you well to "call in well," an illness is created to give you an excuse to stay home and pursue joy. This principle applies to all illness (see Germs, p. 22).

All illness is the refusal to receive the lesson that the illness represents. There are those of us who feel they have earned their illness. It is the ticket out of here and nothing is going to take it away, but still these individuals consciously "think" that they "want" to get well.

In the mid-1980s a spirit being named Hilarion began giving us information that affords much greater clarity about being an incarnate. To sum up his work briefly: Belief conflicts, "lessons" unremembered and unresolved, are represented by specific ailments. Any problem that has been in place for some time has a thought-form built around it. Identifying these thought-forms/beliefs is the key to releasing the disease.

War: When two countries have a belief conflict, it is called war. Mothers send their sons off to be killed. The object is to outgrow war. The United States is the perfect model of one-world government. You would never hear North Carolina declare war on South Carolina. The Feds would step in. It is time for our planet to form such a one-world government. Then a crisis between any two countries would be adjudicated by the World Government. War on our planet would be no more possible than a war between two individual states in America. The time is now.

Further, our planet cannot even be represented in the Galactic Government until we have a unified voice (and we *know* UFOs are real). The galaxy isn't interested in hearing what chatter the huge number of countries on our planet have to babble. In order for the human family to be heard, we must speak with one voice. We must know what we know.

It looks like half of us are at war with themselves and someone else. The other half are just at war with themselves. The reason there can be war on our planet is that each of us, individually, carries the spark within us that can ignite the fire that is war. When we extinguish the battle within, the battle outside of us will stop. "War is the only enemy," as Capt. Picard (Patrick Stewart) says in the series *Star Trek: The Next Generation.*

The War of Ors

The word *or* creates the illusion of two paths. There is only one. Even though it looks like there are two there is only one. Every decision is simply a breath; decide and you are free.

Language is worded in a way that suggests that the power, in this case the ability to decide the "or," is somehow outside of us. All the information that appears to be "missing" can be downloaded directly through the top of the head instantly by command. (If this appears not to work, it is because we do not yet believe that it can.) We create 100 percent of our lives and that is a huge percent of deciding. Deciding isn't "work," it is just thought.

It is important to recognize the effect of the "or" element in our language. The word *or* literally means that a decision is called for—immediately. That's much different from "the decision is not made yet," which the word *or* might suggest. If we don't make the decision, it is entered as a default code.

We live in word world. We can choose to move more toward thought world. Imagine living on a planet where the name of the planet means "to think." Make the decision and the following words disappear: Boring, Horror, Terror, and Worry.

Boring: This is actually "being the or." Boring is the decision to be vs. the decision to do. The principle is to decide between the "ors."

Horror: This is even more "ors," even more doubt.

Terror: The "or" that tears.

Worry: Worry is a distortion of our natural ability to focus. It appears to have been derived from an overuse of the word *or*. You know this—or that. Like the word *if*, the word *or* was originally created in order to explore options.

Worry is a lack of faith, as it eclipses the decision making process. When we as a race make decisions knowing that the decision will occur without a single doubt, then we will have taken an enormous step forward. As it appears, we believe in external forces that are acting against us. This is such victim mentality. I don't worry because I know that I create the future, and in the process, decide on options. The word *worry* is literally "the war of the ors."

The Language of Manipulation

All manipulation is guilt manipulation. Each and every time we are manipulated, it is because we are acting guilty. There are no exceptions. Guilt is the driving force behind all manipulation.

All of the guilt manipulation devices are fully installed and operational by about age two. Thus, the terrible twos are when the child enters an equal footing with the adult. After that, there is no change in the way we operate. We may like to believe there is more development; however, there is only pseudo-sophistication. These techniques of guilt remain unchanged up until death and then in reincarnation. There is nothing new about manipulation, except what you are about to read.

Never act guilty and you will never be manipulated. As we become aware of the devices that appear to control us, we change the Pavlovian response in ourselves. As long as we believe that we must manipulate in order to ensure survival, we agree to be manipulated. By manipulating we are manipulated. To be a slave master does not mean that one is not a slave. A healed consciousness will not even attract this manipulating sort of energy.

Guilt is the byproduct of the phenomenon of right vs. wrong. To have done something wrong and therefore be guilty is not actually possible. Everything is agreed to and orchestrated in higher realms. By the way, everything may be perfect and still be a work in progress.

Guilt is efficiently described as a feedback loop in the self-judgment/self-punishment anomaly set up on this planet.

Notice that guilt is actually all internal. It doesn't have much to do with the big picture. No matter who says you are guilty, it is really only self-judgment that counts. In our society, at this time, we are guilty for everything all the time. *Rubbish!*

You are not now and never will be guilty. We are all, by our nature, innocent little children playing. This is the truth! We are taught to act guilty from day one. We are taught to judge, and to judge ourselves most of all. In spite of the rumors spread by the church, in spite of the relentless brainwashing/programming that appears to be ongoing, I'm born innocent and so are you. Shall we act like it? Let's stop defending ourselves. Start living life. Any time you find a "guilty little thought," eradicate it immediately and reset with loving thoughts. We free ourselves (see Original Sin, p. 31).

Personally I took pen in hand and wrote 5,000 times, "I remember who it is I really am." I must say information is still downloading from this affirmation. So much so that my solar plexus hasn't felt "guilt" in a long time.

We agreed to this walk through sin in order to become wise. After we egress from this state of guilt, we again become innocent. This is not the same innocence; we are innocent and wise at the same time. Now that's evolution!

Guilt, fear, and worry are all the same thing. They are the *only* cause of illness, death, and loss of hair on our planet. We can be-lame germs or genes, we can dance "worst case," and we can pretend that "we have no power," but it doesn't serve us, and it is a very boring way of life. Guilt is the past tense of fear. Love cannot actually be destroyed by guilt. It may, however, appear to vanish it behind the veil.

What is the thing that you are most ashamed of in your life? Come back now, in the present. You see now that whatever that thing is, it assists you to become more compassionate. In this sense, guilt serves a higher purpose, so thank it, honor it, praise it, love it for its service—and be done with it. We no longer have to be guilty for serving a higher purpose.

Let's come back to the idea of acting guilty. Take a look at the night before the crucifixion trial of Christ. Can you picture Christ sitting there thinking something like, "If I can just get the right lawyer, I can get it reduced to flogging served." Christ is not guilty and did not act guilty. He defended himself with perfection. He didn't say a word. If someone even says, "I'm not guilty," it is acting guilty. Besides, defending always sounds like whining.

As we said, acting guilty opens you to manipulation. Our mind has been trained from birth to be easily manipulated. If someone hits another with certain words, this person may go into shock and become unconscious. While unconscious, the subconscious goes on automatic pilot. The subconscious then begins acting out whatever programming is current. This usually means we are really open to manipulation.

Guilt is the linchpin for the language of manipulation. The idea is to place the attention of the manipulatee on guilt. The manipulatee will then leave the now, going to the place of guilt or imaginary debt. Once this happens, the manipulator can put in any suggestion. When we remember we are not guilty, then we don't act guilty, and we are therefore untouched.

Watch it happen: Guilt triggers the predator every time. When the gazelle runs, the predator attacks. There is the confrontation, and the victim decides not that they are weaker, but that they *believe* they are. The retreat, the flight, signals the carnivore to pounce. Were the gazelle to ignore the predator, there would be no cue to attack. The predator wouldn't trigger.

We who read this book, we who are becoming individually God conscious, have all come from a place where we are loyal to God. In this place selfishness is a nonissue. Love is a given. There is no concept of lack. When we incarnate here, we are confused and misdirected by words such as *selfish*, *self-centered*, and *self-love*.

The word *selfish* is a term of abuse. Accompanying this term of abuse is the infamous *self-centered*. Excuse me, but where exactly is my center supposed to be located? If we were designed to have our centers somewhere other than ourselves, wouldn't we be called exocentric?

We are brought down here as little blank slates. We are injected with the notion that selfishness is wrong. Selfishness is encrypted as stealing from others. Like all such slavery words, it is used to manipulate.

Selfishness is "lack" mentality because it is predicated on the idea that there isn't enough to go around. It is used to rob us of our support systems. When we are committed to ourselves, it is perfectly all right to do anything that enhances our abilities, our gifts, our creativity. We must nourish ourselves. Once we are nourished we can be in a position to play with others. In playing with others, we support the entire system.

Self-love does not equal selfishness. If I do something nice for someone, the world is a better place to live in. If I do something nice for me, the world is a better place to live in. There is no real difference between love of self and love of others.

The Four Dialects of Guilt

In this section we will explore the language of guilt manipulation. Certain words we use in our relations with others create as guilt what is really self-love. Our language has more guilt, fear, and manipulation devices than some of us are comfortable recognizing. Yet in recognizing these words and consciously discontinuing their use, we have a path to some serious mental freedom. We no longer have to think in words that make us dance like guilty little puppets.

I take this opportunity to thank James Redfield for his modeling of the four "control dramas" in the *Celestine Prophecy*. This modeling has allowed me to understand how the Language of Manipulation is divided into four dialects, plus the larger falsehood of expectation. Overall we are outlining the methods and vocabulary of taking life force from another. The very first concept is that it is not possible to take life force from another. It must be agreed upon and given. So our description here is of the language that puts us to sleep while we give up our life force to another. Stay awake.

The Dialect of Victimese

The language of the victim is Victimese. When we play the role of victim, we are the manipulator. A victim is a person who feels that things are done to them not by them. A fundamental faux pas, as we create 100 percent of our existence. We decide our life. We decide our fate.

Victims in one way or another ask you to take care of them because, well, they're too busy being a victim to do it for themselves. Beware the whine tone; it means you are being manipulated. When you hear the whine tone say, "Mommy (Daddy) doesn't hear you when you whine." This technique may totally derail the manipulator, who in this case looks like the victim.

The concept is to make you guilty because of manipulators' "problems." Guilty of not being a friend? Guilty of being "selfish," and therefore not having time to solve their problems for them. A true friend, someone who is assigned to watch another's back, would be supportive by *not* rushing in and solving the problems. Allow others to provide for themselves. This is a definition of a friend, and the job description called "parent." We raise adults, not children, as in "Adult Children of Alcoholics." Hear how the language takes the power of people who seek assistance through this particular support group?

The moment we realize that we choose what happens in our life is when we stop being the victim of what happens in our life. Observe the difference between being the victim and being the creator.

LANGUAGE THAT SUPPORTS
THE ILLUSION OF THE VICTIM

Abandon: To believe the word *abandon* is to generate low self-esteem. To feel abandoned is to feel that we are less because someone else no longer places his or her attention on us. The amount of pain we experience is in proportion to how long it takes us to remember that we create our experiences. Think of a world in which our sense of self-worth is not codependent on the attention or opinion of another, where we find all we desire, regardless of whether people move on and "abandon" us.

We may create the experience of being abandoned. This will turn out to be us creating our own freedom. For another to play the role of someone who abandons us, we would have to pretend to abandon ourselves as reaction; it would generate the illusion of worthlessness, pain. Simply, this is nonsense. When we realize that we would never abandon ourselves and therefore could not possibly be abandoned by another, even if the play looked this way, we discover it to be evolution. Evolution equals adaptation. Adaptation equals self-reliance. Being self-existing, yet within the structure of civilization, is the future.

The concept that we create 100 percent of our life, the idea that we have all of the resources to create everything we desire, will not fit into the same head with the concept of being abandoned. Choose.

Annoyed: This word is more accurately spelled *a-noid*. This is noid as in humanoid. So we lose our beautiful hue when we become "a noid." This is literal, in that the color of our aura is affected exponentially by our mood. The hue in question stands for hue-more (humor), as well. Funny eh?

To say "annoyance" is to say "bug," and more specifically, the fly. To foster a greater understanding of our universe is to know the service that the common housefly provides. These marvelous little beings are harmonically tuned to annoyance. The more annoyed one is, the more attractive we become to this divine little being. Thanks, universe, we now have a fly detector.

Betrayal: This is abandonment with a specific action against a preconceived agreement. Consider that anything appearing to be against one is ultimately going to turnout to be in favor of one.

The preconceived agreement would be discussed and rewritten were it not for the popularity of codependency—in other words, were we not afraid of the other person hurting him- or herself. We could say that the relationship, the agreement, is coming close to completing itself. We will be continuing on diverse paths. Free of codependency, *betrayal* becomes *renegotiations*.

Betrayal is where we lie to a person because we still have feelings for them! Thinking with a word like *betrayal* works very much against us. The only one capable of betraying you is you. You are the only one who can specifically act against you. Even then, it will only create the illusion of delay.

Disturbance: Dis-turbulence is a clearer way to see this concept. First, "Dis" is to have no respect for (thank you, Ebonics). As far as the turbulence goes, who created it? We are not disturbed on the roller coaster. A roller coaster ride, now there is turbulence! We agreed to it and even pay for it. We enjoy this. So let us not forget to enjoy all the free turbulence.

Frustrated: Frustration is possible only when we insist that there is only one acceptable outcome. When we are at ease, we are far less frustrated.

Grief: We are so conditioned to hold on to pain. Notice that the initial shock of grief stops our breath. Like all self-indulgent feelings indicating victimhood, grief has an instant relief. Just breathe and begin the process of recognizing the blessings. The other path (holding on to grief) is like turning a brain to leather—totally locked in a single moment in the time line.

Irritated: Is this irradiated? Perhaps eerily-taunted? Who is doing the taunting? This is where something slowly creeps into our awareness. We did not spare the focus (brain space) to bring it up and banish it. So it turns out that our personal performance (not banishing sooner) is the origin.

Loss: Loss is a trick of the placement of one's sacred attention. To say "loss" is to not put our attention on what gain has occurred, what we still have. Things come, things go. Thinking with the word *loss* may result in yet another anchor in the time line, taking up literally millions of future thoughts. The millions of future thoughts are the larger part of the "loss."

Male-dominated society: This is not a male-dominated society. We live in a victim-mentality society. There are no victims.

Missed opportunities: Since we are always being where we are, doing what we are doing, it is impossible to miss anything. It turns out we are trained to dislike where we are and what we are doing. First it's called homework, then it's just called work.

Naturally we become good at escapism. As a result, there are a lot of us walking around with nobody home. We are always fanaticizing, to say nothing of talking on cell phones. Look at how much brain space a cell phone conversation takes up. People walk right out into traffic because their awareness is on the phone, not on the street.

As another result, we run a thought track concerning what we could be doing. This would be what we are "missing." The resulting comparison game drains what little joy remains in the actual now. Thinking about what we may be missing keeps us from participating, keeps us from recognizing the beneficence in the opportunities we didn't miss (see "The Path of Regret," p. 144).

Revenge, Avenge, Vengeance, Vendetta, and Justice: Someone does something purposefully to hurt another. Then what? We hurt them, and then someone hurts us for hurting them. Then the next generation takes up in exactly the same place. It's been going on since the first guy hit the other guy, thus creating the first hurt guy. "Feud"—now that's a word not to leave the kids!

This whole thing comes to a stop when we decide to change the way we think. Being raised in this environment makes us a little thin skinned. We are trained to be hurt, to look to be hurt. When we are not so easy to hurt, when the buck stops here, when we never hurt our children, we will have time to create an even more magnificent future than just one where nobody ever hurts anyone.

The concept of justice is supposed to put an end to all of the above. Does it? The main difference between the first four words and *justice* is that justice is done "officially," by someone else, someone outside of us. This is to assume there is someone "outside."

Justice was originally a stopgap measure to prevent the primitive us from self-extermination. In other words, someone from clan A disturbs someone from clan B. Then the two clans exterminate each other because of revenge. This results in zero population.

In order to preserve peoplekind, a third clan was invented. Their job was to keep "justice" from killing everyone. Clan C, the police, the system, sees to it that only the one who directly hurt the other is punished. No countenance is given to the overall picture. This bigger picture shows that the one hurting was in turn hurt by those who raised him, who were in turn hurt by those who hurt them, and so on back in time.

In order for justice to be done, someone must be treated unjustly. When we actually stop acting guilty, no one will find any reason to act unjustly toward another. Just to put it in our records, a planet is referred to as civilized once there has been no standing army for eighty generations. This can be accomplished, because everybody on such a planet is raised in a way that they are self-regulating, self-sovereign. On these planets, the concept of government has become internal instead of external.

As cohost of Telepathic TV Mary Phelan points out, "justice equals peace." To truly transmute the situation is to find peace within oneself.

Taken, Theft, Stolen: After being robbed, one is better educated. Observe the education that we experience as a result of a theft. All things are love. Not to deride, not to condone, instead to thank the thief, because this individual has helped in some way. We live a different life. The amount of time taken to recognize the gain, the blessings, is the choice of the individual. No matter what has been taken, it will return, if we choose to call it.

Look at this act of being robbed as movement forward, just like everything else. Another choice: you may fixate on the "loss." Not so productive, is it? To heal this situation is to relanguage the things stolen as a "tuition paid." Whatever was stolen is equal in value to the recognition of our own worth, own creativity, which is ultimately the result. Tuition or loss, choose. Another thing that may be said of thieves: they lighten our load.

THE VICTIM AS THE SACRED GEOMETRIC FORM OF THE TRIANGLE

When we create life as a victim, there must be an attacker, an antagonist, a predator. So our victim is always seeking a rescuer as well as creating a villain. This is an incredible work of manifestation. What power, seemingly misused, yet nonetheless, what power. If one is a rescuer, one is still of the victim genus. The same principle applies to the persecutor. In other words, whichever of these three roles one plays, one is playing with victim mentality.

To actually assist people who speak Victimese at you, you redirect their attention to the fact that they have the solution easily at hand within their own camp. If they refuse to hear, then your job is done; walk away. This idea of walking away is the gift called "Duty Done." To leave people to marshal their own resources is an act of kindness.

Healed victims are people who know that they have all of what they require, in fact, more than they require—a philanthropist. The movie *Pay It Forward* is the first modeling of a healed victim as a champion that I've ever seen. In case you fell for the disclaimer at the end of the story, the death of one of the main characters, death is the big reward, not loss. In fact, it is the really big reward, so the kid got his gift.

Healed persecutors are people who know they have all that is required, in fact, more. Once the realization comes that we don't have to take from others or direct anyone's behavior save our own, we become free. The aggression of the persecutor then transmutes into the warrior for the light.

Healed enablers, rescuers, first come to the realization that they must let others take care of themselves. An excellent way to make everyone happy is to not take "responsibility" for whether or not other people are happy. This is the action of love they have been seeking on behalf of the other. When we have children, it is our privilege as parents to assist them to become successful adults. The healed enabler is the loving parent, the nurturer. We are all always in contact with our own internal connection to the Source. Happy self-parenting!

VICTIMESE AS THE LANGUAGING
OF THE BROKEN HEART

A broken heart is feeling incomplete, somehow less than whole without the one loved. Watch the process unfold: First the sorrow becomes the inquisition. How was I wrong? How will I find my other teachers? How can I cope? This list has two qualities: It's endless and it's boring.

All of the languaging necessary to create a broken heart has one thing in common. It is all in the past tense! Does this convey the message? In the past tense is where we are not.

The mending is how long "what could have been" remains interesting. How long can "what could have been" hold the attention? Creating possible futures from the perspective of one moment in the past is counterproductive at best. What is? Here is passion. The glorious me, here in the Now!

The broken heart: How will I ever get along without what's their name? How will I ever find my teachers? These mythical fears give the voice that special whine, and soon all your friends are not returning your phone calls.

Closure: As we have said before, we use the word *sure* to convince (see Doubt, p. 16). The person desiring closure is the one who is convincing him- or herself. Clo-sure is where we believe that the other person must, in some way, give approval before we are comfortable enough to move on with life. Whether or not we get confirmation from the out-side, it is just like validation (see Validation, p. 91), it is the internal system that issues the go. "I am closure."

Rescue: In giving up your personal victimhood, do not res-cue others. The reason is that you become entangled in the rescue mentality. As long as you don't rescue, you don't attract having to be rescued.

Sentimental: Sent I my mental. Sent I my mind, where? Past, future, so long as we are not in the now we aren't in power. Careful where you send your mental. It is handy in the now. The word could be spelled *semi-mental* in that a huge percent of the mental is not there. Demi-mental? No, there is far less than half a brain. How about mini-mental?

Soul mate: Soul mate is inherently plural. In each lifetime we meet and love many, many soul mates. Some are male, some are female, some are animal. In fact, there is no being in the universe that we are not soul-mated with.

In the recognition that each of us creates our own life, it becomes apparent that we are each our own true soul mate. You will spend the rest of your life with you; you are the one who will share in all the experiences on your path. The idea that our power, our mate, for that matter anything else, is outside of us is a very primitive way to think. Without this term *soul mate* we would be all be free to enjoy everything that happens.

The concept of a soul mate is really another way of thinking in terms of ownership, "my soul mate." It is another word of measurement, in other words, it only causes pain and paranoid territorialism.

The Dialect of Inquisition

The principle of the three roles, three archetypes, of persecutor, victim, and rescuer applies to the other dialects of manipulation as well. In the Dialect of Inquisition, persecutors are the ones who ask the questions, victims are the ones who don't know they are not required to answer the questions, and rescuers are the ones who tell the victims that they don't have to answer. When people question us, they are arbitrarily placing themselves in charge of where our sacred attention is placed. Just reply, "No, thanks."

The word *interrogation* is more easily recognized in its original hyphenated form: in-terror-gating. It is my opinion that if other people do not volunteer information about where they were or what they were doing, then it is to be regarded as not my business. Therefore it is not interesting. Knowing would not serve me.

It is a matter of etiquette, privacy, and personal space. Considering people to owe an accountability for their deeds or time is to believe in ownership. The idea of owning another is commonly referred to as slavery. We may decide to volunteer our whereabouts by choice, even with joy about our accomplishment.

All questions are rhetorical. The answer is encoded in the question itself. As in, "Is this the right person?" Were it not for the doubting subtext of our language, such a question wouldn't come up unless he or she was indeed not the person. Even in basic civil questions, such as "Is this seat taken?" the answer is obvious. If there is no one in the seat, it isn't taken. Were someone holding it for another person, it is up to them to speak up. Then one may reply, "I will yield the seat when the reservee arrives."

The question mark itself proves the point perfectly. It is a hook. Unless one is enlightened, as soon as a question is asked, a hook goes in. As we grow in our consciousness, the hook doesn't even penetrate the outermost layers of our auric field.

All questions are a form of doubt. All questions are decisions as yet unmade. Some people think they have questions about their future. If you have a question, it really means a decision has not been made yet. Make the decision. Don't confuse a doubt with a question. For many years people have asked me to use my psychic powers to look into the future to answer some question or other. What is actually going on is that the person has not made a decision. They have not yet chosen which future to create, and they are telling me this in the form of a question, as though this is some gigantic game of *Jeopardy*.

Now, I may pretend that I am indeed the World's Greatest Psychic and proceed to make up some answer or other. Then they may, as a result, actually place their attention on my suggestion. And by placing their attention on it, they actually make it manifest. Then they have a body of evidence indicating that I am most assuredly the World's Greatest Psychic. Actually, no real evidence has been gathered. Like all superstitious thought, it is no more than placing one's attention and growing a belief. Said belief then creates the events.

Further, if I were to give them a timetable by "predicting" a date, then my accuracy would be described as uncanny. While all the time the person is creating their reality themselves. And at the same time crediting me with it.

This is a description of a superstitious mind. The reason

you bought this book is to outgrow such thinking and finally become conscious instead of being superstitious. Let's continue by realizing the answer to the question and the decision about the question are the same thing. As soon as you decide you know the answer, the answer becomes known. It has nothing to do with the future.

Questioning is codependence. Reply, "I would have volunteered the information were it any of your business." When one is used to questioning and someone replies "not your business," the inquisitor hears the rebellion of the slaves. They are likely to engage in the most stringent guilt manipulation. It can be quite entertaining, unless one believes it.

LANGUAGE THAT SUPPORTS THE INQUISITOR

How: As soon as we hear "how," we are in the presence of a technique freak. Being concerned with technique keeps us from being the answer and demotes us to human doing. There is one technique: to be.

"May I ask?": This is asking for your permission to be probed. It lowers your perimeter. Reply: "No."

"What's all this then?": Again, assuming we are not engaged in conversation with an English bobby—perhaps even if we are—the question reply works, as in, "What do you think?"

Why, What, Where, and When: As statements these words serve us. As questions they have a certain amnesia associated. They are the basics of all questioning. These words are useful devices in organizing a plot, a story line. Questioning habituates us to the notion of power as something outside of us.

When someone asks "why" all the time, even when this person knows the answer, and you call him on it and he says it's just for "confirmation," you know a lot about this individual. Little children go through a period where they are always asking why, why, why. The adult who does this was traumatized at this epoch of development. He or she has forgotten their knowing. Just keep repeating "You know why." Those of us always asking what, where, and when have also forgotten our internal knowing.

Questioning is deciding. Once it is decided, it becomes. Decide.

"You must answer.": This is the inquisitor acting like a bully. The reply to this question in the form of a sentence: "I am the only one who says what I have to do."

The Dialect of Elitism

The term *elite* doesn't just refer to people with a superiority complex, it is a concept inherent in our way of life. The healing of it starts with the realization that we are all equal to each other. We are all just volunteers who agreed to forget that we are God. There is no possibility of an elitist being an elitist without the cooperation of the "inferior," the "victim." The idea of one being better than another is a byproduct of the comparison game. No one wins the comparison game.

The elitist is always in a state of expectation of others. It is the nature of codependence. We no longer have to do this when the expectation is in our own performance, not the performance of others.

LANGUAGE THAT SUPPORTS THE ILLUSION OF THE ELITIST

Apology: There are three forms of apology. The first is the social apology. This is the "I'm sorry," when we brush against a stranger. This form of apology is more of a worthiness issue, it does not serve us well. The second form is to prevent further damage being done by the one apologized to; this is fearful and insincere. It only appears to serve well, because the source of the abrasion is not resolved. The third apology is where we truly recognize our role in the event. When we apologize in this sincere way, we are flooded with release, which comes in the form of gratitude. When people are obdurate, refusing to ever apologize, they cut themselves off from gratitude.

At least: The basic "elite" premise is that someone is obliged to come up to the standards set by the elitist. It just isn't true. The latest replies include: "Talk to the hand," and the ever popular, "You aren't the boss of me."

Compassion vs. Enabling: When we give someone the means by which to continue their life, it is compassion. When we do not give someone the means by which to continue their life, this is also compassion. This is because they will find their own resources to continue their life. All enabling is compassion; not all compassion is enabling. All of us have, already, 100 percent of what is required to lead a beautiful life. Enabling is an elitist concept; compassion is not.

Controversial: "Control-reversal." Something that is controversial is contrary to control. It is something we have no place for in our thinking. We have to build one. Controversial means it must be thought about. It also means to do your own thinking about it.

Diploma: Why do you think they call it a sheep skin? I am in no way speaking against self-improvement. What I am saying is that we can widen our acceptance of valid behavior. The proof of our validity hangs on our wall only if we are an artist. People who are an authority, who know something, carry their credentials in their auric field. Eye contact reveals the individual's competency in an instant.

Earn: "Ear-n(ot)," in other words, not to hear. Love cannot be earned, and there is only love. We have unmasked the word *learn* (see Learn, p. 28). *Earn* is like *learn* except associated with work, and work is a word of masochism.

Goal: The thing about a goal is that one drops out of warp at the moment the goal is achieved. There is no planning for life postgoal. For example, if someone sets a goal weight, when it is achieved all the artificial discipline fostered by the program dissolves, and the binge takes over.

We are not against achievement. The idea is that the "goal" is the byproduct of a much greater mandate. In other words, it's not diet or self-deprivation that moves us to the ideal weight; it is the byproduct of the decision to be a healthier, better person. The goal will serve us only as one stepping stone in a long journey. The way the word *goal* is used it means "the end." There is no more instruction after the "goal," and who knows what might happen without our hand at our own rudder.

"I'll take care of you.": This really means "I'll control you." The presumption is that the person does not have the capacity to take care of him- or herself.

This is the active intervening in people's lives, preventing them from taking care of themselves by doing it for them. When we feel in charge of the happiness of others, we become controlling. In doing this, we place their happiness outside of themselves. It may be spoken as a person's happiness being contingent upon the actions, mood, outcome of someone else. This is an unnecessarily vulnerable position.

In entering the elite position of caretaker of another, we take our charge off of his or her own course. We all do better taking care of ourselves, bearing in mind, our relationship with the rest of humanity.

When someone is raised by control freaks, that person will either conform, become an ingrate (see Ingrate, p. 137), or heal and unfold the creativity that is unique to us all as individuals. When this person, raised in a controlling environment, becomes frightened, he or she will seek anything that will take control. This puts this individual in a fictitious situation, because we, each of us, control ourselves.

Inappropriate, Appropriate: Both of these words have identical meaning because there is nothing that is inappropriate. I am not saying we allow abuse to be attracted to ourselves. What I am saying is the words are a trick. They are as obsolete as right and wrong. Everything is appropriate. If we call something inappropriate we are just saying that it is outside of our comfort zone, that there has been a failure in the recognition of divine order, the perfection in all things. Both words are abusive. Their use involves separation and guilt manipulation.

These two words are the good cop/bad cop of our vocabulary. They used to be undercover. Whenever used, you are under arrest. You have your behavior being dictated. You are made minion of another's opinion of you.

Appropriate has literally no meaning when examined for intent. There is no one among us who does not behave appropriately for being themselves.

"Proper" and "improper" have been used in exactly the same way. Without a doubt they are the dark side's backup system and equally devoid of anything other that elitism and abuse. People who use them unabatedly will die from staying in their comfort zone.

Ingrate: Ingrates are people whom we have cooperated with (taken emotional responsibility for) and who now will not cooperate with us (allow themselves to be controlled.) To move beyond *ingrate* is to release the drama and get on with our own life.

-Isms—Racism, Genderism, Nationalism, etc.: As long as we, the human family, see ourselves as divided by races, by gender, by what country we are from, by how much money we have, by how good looking, by handicap, and so on, we fall for the bait big-time. As long as we play the be-lame game and fight among ourselves, we are distracted, put to sleep. We are not seeing the big picture. This whole way of life is no longer interesting.

Remember that there is no person on our planet who is not our cousin, period. All animals are our cousins just once removed. The big truth is every human on this planet is enslaved. There are no real exceptions. Just because a person is a slave driver doesn't mean he or she is not enslaved. We could wax romantic and say it was an eco-nomic slavery, or even more dramatically a "spirit slavery." Our souls are not what is enslaved; it is our minds and therefore our bodies and therefore our lives.

There is only one form of slavery. This is the slavery of fear. All races, everyone, has it. John D. Rockefeller died sur-rounded by armed Pinkerton guards because he was *afraid* that angry people would beat him to death, like Frankenstein's monster, when the villagers attacked with torches and pitchforks.

Realize that we are all, each of us, a member of the same family. Make a personal decision on the subject of "isms." If one of us does this, decides to live a life that is not based on "isms," it shows the way for the rest of us (see Ageism, p. 162).

Lunatic: We're all influenced by the moon. Those of us who know it and develop it are in advance of those who don't. To call someone a lunatic is a compliment, the person is acknowl-edging synchronicity with our lunar neighbor. It means: "You have great abilities as a seer, mystic, and medium."

"Make up your own mind.": When someone tells us to make up our own mind, we are being manipulated in exactly the same way our parents manipulated us when we were seven years old. It sounds very much like they are allowing us to make our own choice, but they know you'll make the right choice, which is of course the manipulator's choice.

Obviously: Is this one obvious? Its subtext calls the listener an idiot. Replace with the concept of easily transparent, apparently, seemingly.

Only: "Only 144,000 will be saved." The famous phrase, "Members Only." "Only I can save you." "The only way to get into heaven is . . . ." As soon as the word *only* is used you may know that there is elitism involved. The form that the box is constructed in is: "There is only one correct answer." Did the word *only* in the last sentence set off a sensor? This is another word designed to disconnect us from our pursuit of a greater knowing. It is a shutdown code in exactly the same construct as the nonexistent words (see "Nonexistent Words," p. 104). In healing our language one may refer to something as a singularity.

Tattoo: For some of us, there is the idea that we are not good enough on our own. The idea that we will not be recognized being just ourselves. We then seek validation by applying external symbols—the tattoo, the piercing, the Ph.D.—and once we have it, we then fall to the other side, becoming the elitist and feeling that we are better than other people. These devices brag to everyone about pain endured, educational experience, etc., in short, doing. This is why the word *tattoo* is in this dialect. Hanging initials after one's name is from this same root. One is not good enough to be recognized just by oneself.

Teenager: The word is absolutely debilitating. "Wait until you're older, then you'll understand." If one is curious, then one is old enough. *Teenager* is synonymous with *powerless*. "Puppy love" actually refers to a pure love; it is not nothing, and it doesn't really "go away." (Turns out a "crush" is literal.)

Usually, Naturally, Normally: One of the elitist's methods of compelling guilt is to get people to compare themselves to an imaginary standard. Then they are guilty of not being normal. Personally I'm not so normal, and this I like. Just because a word is compelling doesn't mean that one is compelled.

The Dialect of the Bully

Bullying occurs when our divinity is suppressed. It can be very subtle. The bully is the last resort of the smaller mind. The bully desires to drain our life force. By remembering that everything is done by us rather than to us, by remembering this soul is incapable of going beyond where he or she is at this point, one doesn't give up life force.

All bullies have low self-esteem, which is why they search for a passive victim. The less passive you are, the less likely you are to be bullied. Low self-esteem is the chink in the armor. Ask the bully who picked on him when he was vulnerable. Perhaps this was brought in from a past life. Maybe this is the life where the cycle is broken.

LANGUAGE THAT SUPPORTS
THE ILLUSION OF THE BULLY

Available: This would be someone looking to have a veil thrown over them. Personally, enough with veils.

Complain: "Common pain." The word *complain* is used by a victim who is bullying. The act of complaint is an act of last resort. If all we have left is to complain, then we have forgotten all our power, our self-love. Get over it. Get on it. Do something about it. Inside equals outside, and this is all circumstances, all the time. "Inside equals outside" is our power.

   Instead of complaining, change the inner self, and then the "outside," the life, will have to change. All complaining is taking, whatever the complaint is about personally. It shows a lack of faith in our own power. (This is why all complaint has such a whine tone.) If all resources appear to be exhausted, perhaps not all resources have been recognized.

Inevitable: The only thing inevitable is love. If you use it for anything else, you cloud the mind. In this universe there is always choice.

Repeating: When someone repeats the same thing more than once, this person is attempting to convince us of his or her point of view. It's no one's job to convince us of anything. It is our job. In our unawakened state, we may act guilty and comply. This path does not lead as directly to finding our own opinion.

Sure: As in "I'm sure." *Sure* is used to convince. We may not be sure who is being convinced—the speaker or the listener—but someone is. Listen when you happen to use it. Who are you convincing? It may look like someone else, but it's you talking to you. When you say "sure," it means you're unsure. This really unmasks insurance salesmen.

"That's the way it is.": Each of us individually determines the way it is for us. Your beliefs create your reality! You may say to the tormenter who says this: "That's the way it is for *you*."

"You have no choice.": This phrase is always used to force something. It's a lie. Choice, by definition, is a plural. You always have many choices. One reply: "You may not call yourself my friend and tell me that I have no choice."

BULLYESE AS THE DIALECT OF ANGER

When we become so angry that people cannot talk to us, we are gone. When rage takes us to the point that we don't recognize those who love us, we are gone. To become angry is to slip into a form of dementia. To live a life where we give into the self-indulgence of being angry is to live like an Alzheimer's patient. If you know someone with this disease, you know how at first there is the slip into it and then back out of it. It's just like this with anger. "How long was I gone this time?"

There is no anger; there is only fear masquerading as anger. Anger will be instantaneously revealed as fear the moment you ask, in the words of Carla Neff Gordon on Telepathic TV, "What am I so afraid of that I am choosing anger?"

Make the decision to spend a life dealing with the fear directly, efficiently. When one masters anger by asking the fear to identify itself, it will be revealed that anger always involves judging one's performance. All anger is anger with the self. "Angry" may therefore be spoken as: "acting guilty about judging my performance." Anger is the spike, and "disappointment" (self-judgment) is the valley.

SWEAR WORDS

Swearing is intimidation. If a person uses swearing to express being under some kind of "stress," then the question "Is this person dangerous?" is no longer a question. We back off when someone swears.

We start swearing to get a rise out of those around us. It is a method of "controlling" our environment. Usually one outgrows it. It is just one more face of the frightened bully.

The Charmed Life

To not be guilty, to in fact have a sense of one's own worth, is charming. In order to not be manipulated in any way (to not act guilty), we must not manipulate others, no matter how good we are at it. This is the essence of it. We teach the language of manipulation to recognize and discard its devices, *not to use it*! Manipulator, manipulated, either way one is down for the count.

When we are in no way distracted by manipulation, it will be because we no longer think or act in lack. Think of this state of mind. Remembering our divinity—what a concept! What will our thoughts be like. What sort of life shall we decide to live? It will be our choice; it is our choice.

We are making a path into a world where it is all right, and also a right, to no longer be guilty. This is to say, it's OK to constantly pursue joy, to self-actualize, to play in our divinity. As a step in this direction, we would suggest that there are always millions of things that one may do that are quite enjoyable. If one were to always be doing something on this list and, at the same time, be vigilant of the feelings of others, one would be applauded quite roundly and called a genius. For example, right now I could be doing many other things that would bring joy. Since some number of pages have been written (and by now read by you), I will write the rest of this volume. This is the creation of happiness and the consideration of others.

To be charming is to be loving. The word *charisma* means Christlike. When one is in a state of bliss, recognizing the divinity in all things, one is charming. When one doubts, when one is angry, one is not charming. This is how to lead a charmed life. Of course, one has to know that one can live a charmed life. Then one must make the decision.

The Path of Regret

We walk the path of regret when we consider a path, then do not take it, but then do not let go of it. Each step we take in our current life is compared to a step that "could have been" on the other path. Nothing can ever register at 100 percent.

The path of regret has a recognizable vocabulary. It's full of false words: "should," "mistake," "accident," "If I were your age, I'd . . . ." Recognizing the words is one thing. Removing the ingrained thinking that the words represent is . . . great.

A friend once told me, "We come here to evolve. We evolve by having experiences. We do not judge that we evolve, why judge the experiences?" The moment you regret is the moment you fail to recognize your true intent in the situation. Furthermore, everything that happens is by divine intent, which, if you look carefully, is everyone's intent. The walk on the path of regretlessness is a walk in the land beyond right and wrong. In one sentence: *We walk the path of regret until we recognize the divinity in our decision.*

TAPE LOOPS

Thinking the same thought over and over again destroys the thought efficiency quotient. It may be that we do not yet have the tools to dismantle such a life-sucking mental faculty. Stand by; we are about to create them.

The tape begins when we do something we don't care for. The way we have been taught to think, it looks like someone did something to us. Actually it was our performance during the event that has stuck it in our craw.

Whenever you have a "regret," or you "resent" something, you set up a tape loop. The idea is to watch for thoughts with this false vibrato. They just go round and round like a tape loop. For example, if we hate someone for cutting us off in traffic, the event turns over in our mind again and again. We fall asleep drained of our last ounce of energy by thinking of mashing their molecules again and again.

This energy is very life-destroying negative vitality. Think of what we could be thinking instead of this merry-go-round of lack of self-sovereignty. What a loss of potential (especially considering what a human mind is capable of.) Whoever did whatever; so what! Dismiss it. Actually, thank that person; after all, he is the one who helped wake us.

TAPE LOOP TELEPATHY CONVERTER

We human beings are far more telepathic than is known to us. If you are thinking a tape loop, the one you are thinking about is also thinking. They are thinking their tape loop as well. When you resolve your tape by realizing that it is *your performance* in the event that is causing the static, "t-mail" this to the other. This makes a difference in the other's thinking; and it will be the final touch in your letting go. This is a factor in the permanent healing of your self, so that this loop will never again take up your attention. Then you will not have to do this all night in dreams. The dream time will then be used for other important things.

QUADRANT

4

ARCHETYPE UPGRADE

ARCHETYPES ARE AN IMPORTANT part of our evolutionary process. They are the coding that tells the system how and in what direction to change. An archetype is a gate, a door through which many people pass. It's like a keystone in an arch. It holds a form in place, a portal open, for others to enter.

The first monkey of the one-hundred-monkeys effect is an archetype. The next ninety-eight monkeys then enter the gate. The one hundredth monkey is the launch code, the new archetype for all the other monkeys on the planet that are standing by.

In this book we are presenting new modeling for our use of language, new words and ways of thinking about words that serve as archetypes. Archetypal words and thoughts open spirals upward. They inspire. These words and thoughts become ingrained in the thinking of others, changing the language we all use, and thus the lives of all on the planet. There are always those born among us who choose to show the rest of us the way.

In this chapter we explore modes of thinking and how they shape and are shaped by our language. Life is a way of thought. As we grow new ways of thought, great vistas will appear. There is no human being on this planet that does not have the access codes to other dimensions. Ask the seeds of far greater consciousness that exist within your heart right now to germinate. Grow them with an unyielding quest for new thinking!

Modalities of Thought

There are significantly different models of thought. Certainly the thinking that occurs while we sleep is different from waking thought. These different types of thinking are all serving us well, each in its own way. We are always better off when we acknowledge that there is more than one correct answer—in this case, more than one method of thought. The more we become aware of the different modalities of thought, the greater the scope of our personal thoughts/power. How vast is the array of human thought? Each of us has a unique and wonderfully exciting facet of it.

MONO-THOUGHT

Mono-thinking is going through life with the idea that there is one and only one correct answer. This limits our thinking. One might say, "I have found the one correct answer; therefore, I have clarity." Truly, this is one clarity. In the great abstraction there is only God and therefore there is validity in this.

Nonetheless, there is always more than one correct answer. This is the effect of the multidimensional reality. There are many facets to everything. They are all correct.

Each of us has a personal truth. Therefore, there are 7 billion correct "truths," on the planet and each one is true. Rather than disagree with someone else's truth, to allow polite conversation, we might say one aspect of it is this, and another facet of it is something else. In this way we may present our truth without so much confrontation.

If we consider the word *fact* and add the *e* to it, it becomes *facet*. The *e* is the universal energy. It is symbolized in the spiral nature of the character. Add the universe to a fact and one comes up with a facet.

POLAR THINKING

We are also schooled to believe that we exist in a world of opposites. This significantly affects our reality. Until we outgrow this, we are pulled from one pole to the other throughout our lives. We run a course where first we love it, then we hate it, then we love it, then we hate it. Polarities actually lack balance. It never settles in the all-important middle.

In polarity, the whole of thinking is "educated" to search for the opposite. Opposites are taught as the only approach. Thinking with a head full of opposites may render one with oppositional personality disorder or bipolar disorder. This accounts for the extremes that are apparent in our society. "One extreme to the other." In polar thinking, living it up will result in living it down.

Polar thinking is not reality; it is more like entry-level thinking for the third dimension. Duality, polarity is more of a two-dimensional form of thought. Where does one go from polarity thinking?

TRIANGULATED THINKING

For any two opposites there is a third concept, a third word that balances. Hot and cold are the same because they are both temperature. Red and green are both colors. Triangulate the entire vocabulary.

A car battery is certainly polarized. When we triangulate it, the car starts. In triangulating the mind, we will eventually come to the idea of right and wrong. Right and wrong triangulate at the moment we realize that what they have in common is that they are both a state of existence. They are the arms of judgment, and when we outgrow judgment, right and wrong don't really exist. Something isn't right or wrong; it simply is (see Right and wrong, p. 36).

With our entrance into the world of triangulated thought, a part of us called The Objective Witness sees to an authentic balance in our lives. When we see through the eyes of this part of ourselves—the part that is not invested in who is winning/losing—we see a calm, very effective life. Right now, look at you reading this book. You are seeing you as your objective witness sees you, and I might add, you wear it well. In Sanskrit this is called *advaita*, the nonduality.

SUPERSTITIOUS THINKING

Superstitious thinking is done by a superstitious mind. The seed is planted when grandma tells the kids to spill salt and then have a misfortune. I know that grandma said "*if* you spill salt," but we're talking about the human mind here. The kids then proceed to spill salt and then create a misfortune. Since all of their chums do the same thing, there is created a "body of evidence," which grows the idea that this is true.

By the time this repeats a few generations, the mythos is now on gene level. Since belief creates reality, superstitious thinking just grows a greater body of evidence. The only thing that has actually been proven is that, as author Drunvalo Melchizedek says, "Thought creates and where you place your attention grows."

All superstition is predicated on the idea that there are outside forces that must be courted in order to live a "safe" life. Rubbish! The trick is to remember that there are *no outside forces*! There are only internal forces that appear to be outside forces. If you wish for something to happen, decide that it happens.

Suppose you reach for two sugar packets, but your hand retrieves three. Does this mean that you are destined to have three? Of course not. In this thinking, *chance* and *destiny* appear to have the same definition. Use as much sugar as desired. Decide how much.

Anything that suggests that the creation of one's life is done by anything other than the self is superstitious thinking, as such. There is much more of this thinking than one might realize. Our very concept of God, as it is currently on our planet, is superstition.

RATIONAL THOUGHT

Rational thought is generally defined as steering our way through potential dangers to arrive in a safe place (Where we desire to be). Were it possible to isolate just left brain thinking, without any of the other tools afforded by the human mind, it might be called rational thought.

Here is an example: Human beings, by nature, seek happiness. Judgment always leads to unhappiness. Therefore we are, by our nature, nonjudgmental. So much for logic and rational thought. We "want" happiness. We seek happiness by being unhappy. Judgment equals unhappiness. This is the pox. One could call it insanity; one could call it a good reason to change; one could call it "rational thinking."

Rational thought is paranoia as such. As the beloved Richard Nixon showed us, paranoia is characterized by unnecessary labor. (All of Watergate was unnecessary labor.) Paranoia is further characterized by a pedantic territorialism: keys and locks, war, jealousy, and on and on.

Most of us, at this point, seek to be unhappy approximately one hundredth of a second after arriving at happiness. Our failures hang around our necks like chains holding us in the past, holding us in guilt. Our successes disappear like snow on the water. Reverse these poles! Hang on to happiness and celebrate diversity. It is this simple.

One other note on rational thought. In order to actually map all the variables to steer a course in life, we require a much larger cache of memory than afforded by the human mind. This leads to dependence on clichés—"I didn't see that coming," "Who knew?" or the infamous "cosmic 2 x 4"—as well as all that chatter referred to as worst-case scenario.

"Rational thought" as the only acceptable method of thinking is not serving us well. We are not suggesting giving up rational thought, just adding other types of thinking so that we have a wide range of tools, consciously, at our disposal. All thought has validity in its own way. The idea is whether or not our thinking serves us.

STATISTICAL THINKING, BODY-OF-EVIDENCE THINKING

Mark Twain said it quite well: "There are three types of lies: lies, damn lies, and statistics."

Body-of-evidence thinking is where one accepts statistical information as the "best bet." This limitation is deceptive.

Here is an example of the paralysis created by body-of-evidence thinking: We have a T intersection between two roads. At this intersection 70 percent of the cars make a right turn and 30 percent make a left. There is a car at the intersection; which way will it go? The idea that most of the cars make a right would lead one to "guess" a right turn. Well, with this "body of evidence" our vision is misdirected. Our instincts are off-line. Body-of-evidence thinking only gathers more evidence, it doesn't provide for the conclusion. It blinds the Third Eye (see Skeptic, p. 40).

NONLINEAR THOUGHT

Nonlinear thought, as the name suggests, is thought that does not fall into a line. As logical thinking may describe the process of the left brain, nonlinear thinking is the process of the right brain. It has great potential.

As soon as the concept of the shortest distance between two points is brought up, one may become entrapped in linear thought. The shortest distance between two points is to be at both points at the same time. Thought is the shortest distance between the two points.

This is not logic missing some of the pieces; it is free. Given the straightjacket that is the "normal" thinking that goes on on our planet, most of this book could be described as nonlinear thinking.

INTUITIVE THOUGHT

Intuition always arrives full-blown, without any conscious construct preceding it. (I had a hunch about that.) This type of thinking may be described as the synergy between the left and right brain thinking. It serves us well when it is acknowledged as valid thinking. It could be called knowing without knowing why.

ASSOCIATIVE THINKING

Thinking by association is a cousin of intuitive thought. Associative thinking is the sort of thought that occurs during our dreams. It is more common in our awake time than we may realize. It is the essence of phobia. We don't know why, yet we are afraid of the basement. When the fear is traced to spiders, then we see that the basement is associated with the arachnids and we understand the fear of the basement.

This is why no dream dictionary is right for any individual, unless he or she wrote it. We all have different associations with everything. To interpret a dream symbol, we must first discover what associations we have with it.

Some deride thinking by association with the term *tangential thinking*. Were we to follow these tangents unabashed, who knows where we might go. Find out.

MULTIDIMENSIONAL THOUGHT

Mediumship or channeling is a form of thinking acknowledged by every civilization on our world. The ancients all had oracles to assist the leaders in setting a course. All of us have connection to other dimensions. The ability to set aside the brain and allow information to flow from the higher realms is a talent to be saluted. Each and every one of us has the ability. We all send and receive through it all the time, even when the conscious mind doubts. It's just that the doubt makes the faculty all but useless.

FAILSAFE THINKING

The ability to stop our thinking in midstream is essential to evolutionary thought. It is simply a switch. Practice with the alphabet: A, B, C, D, E, F, G, now stop. The alphabet would have continued, and it stopped. Note this is by your conscious command. All thoughts are this easy to stop. The question is where do we continue our thought stream? If we do not make this decision, H, I , J, K, and so on will be the answer. We have sovereignty over our thoughts as soon as we know it. Set a failsafe for any thought that makes you unhappy. Shut it off the minute it is recognized as "unhappy," for this thought is a fear and therefore unworthy of your sacred attention.

Human Consciousness as the Limitless Creator

We are already limitless creators. We create 100 percent of our life everyday. Many of us realize this. The next step is to live it, to consciously create 100 percent of our life everyday. This is the principle in very simple terms.

A more expanded look involves telling reality what to do and then watching it happen. Say your ride home involves three out of the five traffic lights being red on average. Tell all of them to be green. The universe will obey the command. That is, unless the left brain chatters enough doubt, to keep you from seeing this simple truth. Our beliefs create our reality.

An incarnation in the third dimension is a study of limitation. In order to move on, it will be necessary to master limitation. The mastery of anything involves the love of it. Loving limitation involves realizing that the human power is the ability to generate love. What is there not worth loving? What is there worth giving up power for? Certainly I wouldn't give up my power by not loving limitation. It is after all why we all incarnate here.

Limitless creation is deciding something will happen and then it happens. This occurs owing to a lack of doubt. To ease the doubt, think of a physics text that is over a hundred years old. It would be comedic at best. Think of a physics text from a hundred years in the future. It would be only slightly less comedic. The laws of physics are changing daily, and yet people with no knowledge of them are ruled by them. What nonsense.

Whether or not it is apparent, our life is a series of decisions made by us. Make them consciously. These decisions are not ruled by the laws of "physics." Spend a week of your supposed seventy years of life giving commands and watching what happens. You have been given life; have some fun with it. *All my limitations are inspirations.*

Thought Management

There is one and only one protocol in thought management: "Where am I placing my attention?"

What is the single biggest commodity, in fact the only commodity?

Answer: "Where people are placing their attention."

The single most important thing a human being owns is where the "magic" attention is placed. All of reality is determined by where the attention is placed!

REROUTING

When we become habituated to thinking a certain dark future on a regular basis, we may change these thoughts. It works by writing a program that recognizes the negative thinking and automatically switches "the subject" to a future your prefer. Call it "rerouting." If you always think about debt and going broke, write a program that reroutes the attention to a specific accomplishment instead. Remember that it is guilt that is pulling us toward the Negative Future.

Were we to find ourselves breathing some foul air, thinking of anger, fear, powerlessness, then we may "manage to choose" to place our thoughts on higher ground. Stop reading at this very moment and decide on what a higher thought looks like to you. Do this often. It's called the power of choice. It is inexhaustible.

DECISION BY DEFAULT

Some people feel that managing all the decisions in our lives is too much "work." The thing to realize is that, aware or unaware, all of the decisions in our life are made by us anyhow.

As an example, let's say that we are going to go somewhere that is forty-five minutes away and traffic will be dense because it is 4:30 PM. Observe that every one of those stipulations is a decision made, not "reality." We have still made a series of decisions. We could have decided that the trip will take thirty-five minutes and traffic will be light. Both are series of decisions, the difference is in the belief system. If we do not recognize our power of creation, then the trip is a series of default decisions. When we do recognize that we create our life, then they are just decisions.

Choice as a default code is where we appear to make no firm decision. This is actually not possible. What actually happens is that we give the power of choice to someone else. Default codes are easy to recognize. They all have an air of resignation: "I guess," "I don't care," "Whatever."

It is still your universe directly; however, it will look like other people make decisions for you if you choose the default. For example, if you don't know how to make money, a boss will tell you. Except, he is really telling you how to make money for him, and then he gives you a little. These and all decisions in your life are yours absolutely.

As we have stated, the word *if* is quite capable of taking a decision away from someone. When we say, "If I get there on time," it gives away our power to time. Decide when you get there and it will happen. We have seen this many times. We create time. Recall that the word *if* means make a decision now.

People born on this world are never really told this. Nonetheless it's true. Every decision we make in our life is ours to make. If the sergeant tells you to kill, who pulls the trigger? Who tells your finger to move? What percent of your life do you create?

Tense: The Hidden Language

At the core of how our language structures our thinking is the fear of time. Our language directs—more accurately misdirects—our attention. Words that have tense direct our attention out of the now. As we know, the one and only point of power is in the now. Therefore our language directs us into a state of powerlessness: "Last week I had a good seminar." What happened? Is it now no longer good? We are a species enslaved to time. Decide to stop this *now*.

USE OF TENSE RESULTS IN BEING TENSE

Have you noticed that in the post office there is a clock visible to you the entire time you are in line? Who thought of this?

Time is illusion. When there is a clock involved it is delusion. In the case of language, tense is a delusion.

The object is therefore to speak and think in the present tense. In using tense one does a dissection of the time line. Once seamless in our state of timelessness, things now become separate. "What's happened in the past?" "What will happen in the future?" Think about the now. Now is the place where the power is.

A LIST OF DEFAULT TIME CODES

Adult: Anyone twenty years older than you.

Ageism: It works in either direction: too young, too old, too middle-aged. As we have explained, many invisible languages are built into our words. Age is one. It is a structure of belief, like any other; it is chosen. As we mature, the belief that none of us can beat the clock grows a body of evidence. As always, this sort of thing is done only with our cooperation.

The belief that we grow older is just this, a belief. Count your birthdays backward. Slipstream into a youthfulness. Nostalgia may be more accurately described as "nonstagnation." Surround the self with things that promote your youth-ness. Toys, games, fun generators, call them all!

Are we there yet?: We are here now.

Dog years: This concept is introduced in order to make us feel guilty. What, we are going to outlive the pet, so we give 'em a handy cap? Every pet lives the perfect amount of time. It cannot be done any other way.

Early, Late, On time: Words of abuse. They do nothing but create artificial stress. "Early" and "late" are spoken exclusively to make us wrong. "On time" is often followed by pedantic derision as in, "one is *finally* on time."

These words aren't real. Go ahead; be where you aren't. It isn't possible. If you look through a telescope and Mars isn't where you thought it would be, does that make Mars wrong? No, it means we don't know as much about Mars as we could. We don't have all the info.

When we use words that set up expectation and therefore disappointment, we do not serve ourselves well. In other words, it doesn't work to use these words. Replace them with "My timing is always perfect." Everyone is where they are supposed to be doing what they are doing, regardless of who says what.

Endings and Beginnings: There are no beginnings and endings. It is all a magnificently beautiful spiral. The concept of beginnings and endings is the meat grinder that presents life as chopped up. This paradigm is fueled by the use of tense. We are all drops in the ocean of the universe, and yet we are the universe as well.

Good idea: When we decide that something is a good idea, we create a very special place in our mind. We put it on a "to-do" list, a list of things that would be good to do someday. Of course, someday never comes. To say something is a "good idea" is to say that it won't be done. In fact the more one talks about it, the less likely it becomes. Languaging an idea as a good idea removes it from the now, and therefore it will remain unfunded.

The ability to separate the ideas that will manifest from the plethora of good ideas that pass through our lives may be outlined by the belief one has in the individual idea. We must also believe in ourselves as the one who has decided to be the one who creates this idea.

Good ideas generally serve to outline borders. We put the good idea over there. Great ideas expand the borders of human perception. A good idea is significantly different from a great idea.

Hold and Wait: As in being on hold, "waiting" for a conversation. Hold is the child of waiting. It is used by our negative ego to stop our stream of consciousness, only that doesn't happen. For me, the word *hold* always indicates that I have something else to get in order before I speak to whomever. It is actually an assistance in timing. There is no possibility of being put on hold. Your mind goes on, period.

The way these words are typically used is a distortion of a natural part of the thought process that is called the "gap." For example, if we are in the process of recalling an obscure name and we have (pardon the expression) "racked" our brains to no avail, if we place our attention elsewhere for a while, then the info will come forth. The information appears in the "gap." Note there is no cessation of thought, just attention management. This is taught to children in order to create powerful adults.

Rush, Hurry: *Rush* creates a fear pulse that destroys all joy. These words came into our language based on the idea that we have a limited amount of time to live, or a limited amount of time for anything. There are far greater possibilities than this.

We recall the ancient Buddhist teaching, "If you are late, walk slower." Again, I suggest that thinking in terms of rushing and hurrying be replaced with the concept, "all timing is perfect," and/or "my timing is always perfect."

Starting over again at square one: There is no such thing. All of the experience gained in the first construct plays a key role in the second construct. To quote Data (Brent Spiner) from *Star Trek: The Next Generation*, "There are no failures, there is only more data."

To replace this concept one may say, "Forward to the drawing board," or simply "Reset." Some of us, in our fear, talk about going "back" to something we once did. Believe me there is no such thing. One may go forward to something we did. Don't believe so little in your own worth that you doom yourself to repeat a section of your past. Hit the reset and go forward into the adventure of your future (see "The Path of Regret," p. 144).

Waste of time: How? There is no moment that doesn't move us closer to being a better being. We are creating time. This cliché, "a waste of time," is in the language to make the process appear guilty. Not only is waste impossible, not only do we create time, the universe itself is recycling. It's happening as we read.

LANGUAGING TIMELESSLY

There is no real education on the subject of time on our planet. The first time we hear the word "time" it has the word "bed" in front of it. The next time we hear it, it has "to get up" tacked after it. Then it's time to go to school, time to get a job, time to pay taxes, time to get married, time to get old, time to die. Time is this relentless task master, or so we believe and only for the belief is this true.

Our beloved universe is in a constant state of synergy, all in spiraling cycles. Cycles then recycle and we, in our observation of it, participation with it, create time. All creation is internal cocreation with the external. Therefore we create time in exactly the same way we create all parts of our reality. The more we remember to be in the now, simply the more powerfully we create. Using past and future tense disrupts our relationship with the time line. This, in a real way, interrupts us, our lives.

A great "secret" of writing prose is to have the entire story told in the present tense. It keeps the attention riveted in the now of the story. Our lives are like this. The more in the now one is, the more exciting, the more powerful. This, strangely enough, explains the success of the character Homer Simpson. Despite his simplemindedness, Homer rarely ever leaves the now.

To speak in a language with no tense—here is a concept. If we were raised thinking in a language with no tense, no way to express "not in the now," the concept of tense would seem comical. A native to this non-tense language would wonder why we throw our power away on a fictional time line.

Shall we band together in groups and refer to things that happened in the past as though they are going on in the present? For example, "Last month I am reading this great book. It is helping me remain in the now" instead of "The book *helped* me stay in the now," which is a ridiculous statement. This concept applies to the future also. "My intent is reading this book," rather than, "My intent is to read this book." Our ears are not tuned to such things . . . yet.

No word of power is spoken in past or future tense. Power is now. The only time that anything can be done is now. Planning yes, participation is now.

Brain Language Upgrade

The object of this book is to render each of us capable of noticing exactly what effect any individual word (or thought) may have in the field as well as able to dismiss the useless language. And further, to do this simply by our own authority!

We have a language-sound-decoder in our brain. It is already installed. Initializing it is easy. If there is question about the effect of a particular word, just open its file and look at the effect the word has on the all that is. Words are meant to be our servants, not masters.

It's the filing language our brains use that requires upgrading, and that this book addresses. This is the same language that we speak/think.

For example, if we use a word like *regret* to file with, then whatever we "regret" remains in a file that is never reviewed. It may be commiserated, but never reviewed. Most certainly a regret will never be refiled as a blessing. Even when new info comes in, related to the event, that would upgrade it to a blessing, still nothing is refiled. Filing a thought as a regret is like the dead letter office.

Filing thoughts with the old language system eventually creates pockets of numb or dead brain space. Take a look at your own internal file marked "should." (At least call the whole thing "the could have" listing instead.) Or look at how you are using *hard*, *difficult*, *insult*, *boring*, and so on as categories of experiencing and consequently filing. Notice that everything that has been filed as a fear has a shutdown code tagged to it.

By the time we are ready to go to the next level in our incarnational process, the brain is so jammed with misfiled info that we have to spend hours in that moment where our life flashes in front of our eyes. It is an enormous refiling project.

The really joyous news is that we can upgrade the filing system we think with. Say out loud, "I am the higher languages."

The Power of Our Language Creates

There is a growing curiosity as to exactly what we would be thinking if we weren't so busy being distracted by fictional devices like anger, shame, guilt, and so on. These false words/thoughts are reruns, that are toooo boring to keep watching again and again, much less participate in. When we choose to stop acting guilty, our hearts open, our lives become joyous.

Each new generation forms its own vernacular because we must escape the mind-set of the preceding generation. The newly coined words and expressions are the words of power for the ones who speak them. Our language is alive, always renewing itself.

All of our language cumulatively reflect us. Do we speak more words of joy, affirmation, and comfort or words of fear, pain, and derision. We make this decision every day. Begin to grasp what is true human potential. This book makes it apparent what destruction single words in our thinking can render. Who knows what one awakened human can do.

As we think more effectively we will speak far more effectively. It is not "hard." Effortlessly, effervescently slip into a higher languaging. Just call it to yourself. Choose to speak words of verve, words that soar, terms of excitement, full of fulfillment. Epithets that inhale the breath of life! "Better of choice to you!" (Replaces "good luck.")

Gratefully,

R. Neville Johnston

Certificate of Self-Sovereignty

Within the parameters of the Free Will Experiment, I,

_____,

Officially declare myself Sovereign of my body, mind, and Spirit. I am consciously aware of the following:

- My thoughts create and where I place my attention grows.
- My attention is sacred.
- My beliefs create my reality.
- I choose my beliefs.
- I choose the thoughts in my mind.
- I am relaxed, nonchalant, at ease with myself at all times.
- I create time.
- Everything that happens in my life is in my favor, everything, at all times. I celebrate diversity.
- I see through the illusion of agency and recognize the one true cause.
- I am a limitless creator.

BY THE AUTHORITY OF:

_____ DATE_____

WITNESSED:

_____ DATE_____

SIGNED:

_____ DATE_____

Bibliography

Barks, Coleman. *The Soul of Rumi*. San Francisco: HarperSanFrancisco, 2001.

Braden, Gregg. *Walking Between the Worlds: The Science of Compassion*. N.p.: Radio Bookstore Press, 1997.

Cooke, Maurice Borden. *Hilarion, Body Signs*. Toronto: Marcus Books, 1982.

Essene, Virginia, and Irving Feurst. *Energy Blessings from the Stars: Seven Initiations*. N.p.: S.E.E. Publishing, 1998.

Fiore, Edith. *The Unquiet Dead: A Psychologist Treats Spirit Possession*. New York: Ballantine, 1987.

Fortune, Dion. *Psychic Self-Defense*. York Beach, ME: Red Wheel/Weiser, 1957.

Clow, Barbara Hand. *The Pleiadian Agenda: A New Cosmology for the Age of Light*. Rochester, VT: Bear and Co., 1995.

Hawken, Paul. *The Magic of Findhorn*. New York: Harper and Row, 1975.

Keller, Thomas, and Debrah S. Taylor. *Angels: The Lifting of the Veil*. Charlottesville, VA: Hampton Roads, 1994.

Levitt, Stephen and Stephen Dubner. *Freakonomics*. New York: William Morrow, 2005.

Melchizedek, Drunvalo. *The Ancient Secret of the Flower of Life*. N.p.: Light Technology Publications, 1999.

Men, Hunbatz. *Secrets of Mayan Science/Religion*. Rochester, VT: Bear and Co., 1990.

Orr, Leonard. *Breaking the Death Habit*. Berkeley: North Atlantic Books, 1998.

Ray, Sondra, and Leonard Orr. *Rebirthing in the New Age*. Berkeley: Celestial Arts, 1983.

Redfield, James. *The Celestine Prophecy*. New York: Warner Books, 1993.

Sams, Jamie. *Medicine Cards: The Discovery of Power through the Way of the Animals*. New York: St. Martin's, 1988.

Urantia Foundation. *The Urantia Book*. Chicago: Urantia Foundation.

Walsch, Neale Donald. *Conversations with God: Book 2, An Uncommon Dialogue*. Charlottesville, VA: Hampton Roads, 1997.

Yogananda, Paramahansa. *Autobiography of a Yogi*. Nevada City, CA: Crystal Clarity Publishers, 1946.

About the Author

R. NEVILLE JOHNSTON was shot to death in 1977. He woke up in a hospital able to see people in their past lives. This NDE or "shaman's death" was just the beginning. He believes that he was sent back to assist in raising human consciousness to a higher echelon by helping us learn to speak an ascended language. He is the author of many books including *The Language Codes* and *Telepathic Etiquette*. Johnston lives in Reston, Virginia.

Beloved reader, if you have any questions, you may write to me at 2210 Coppersmith Sq., Reston VA, 20191. You may contact me by telephone at 703-860-2333 or by e-mail at *telepathictv@yahoo.com*. Or visit the site at

www.telepathictv.com

If you have mail, phone, or e-mail, you have a metaphysician.

To Our Readers

WEISER BOOKS, an imprint of Red Wheel/Weiser, publishes books across the entire spectrum of occult and esoteric subjects. Our mission is to publish quality books that will make a difference in people's lives without advocating any one particular path or field of study. We value the integrity, originality, and depth of knowledge of our authors.

Our readers are our most important resource, and we appreciate your input, suggestions, and ideas about what you would like to see published. Please feel free to contact us, to request our latest book catalog, or to be added to our mailing list.

Red Wheel/Weiser, LLC
P.O. Box 612
York Beach, ME 03910-0612
www.redwheelweiser.com